North East Scotland

Edited by Mark Richardson & Annabel Cook

D1350729

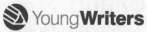 Young**Writers**

First published in Great Britain in 2008 by:
Young Writers
Remus House
Coltsfoot Drive
Peterborough
PE2 9JX
Telephone: 01733 890066
Website: www.youngwriters.co.uk

SB ISBN 978-1 84431 661 8

Foreword

Young Writers was established in 1991 and has been passionately devoted to the promotion of reading and writing in children and young adults ever since. The quest continues today. Young Writers remains as committed to the nurturing of poetic and literary talent as ever.

This year's Young Writers competition has proven as vibrant and dynamic as ever and we are delighted to present a showcase of the best poetry from across the UK and in some cases overseas. Each poem has been selected from a wealth of *Little Laureates 2008* entries before ultimately being published in this, our seventeenth primary school poetry series.

Once again, we have been supremely impressed by the overall quality of the entries we have received. The imagination, energy and creativity which has gone into each young writer's entry made choosing the poems a challenging and often difficult but ultimately hugely rewarding task - the general high standard of the work submitted ensured this opportunity to bring their poetry to a larger appreciative audience.

We sincerely hope you are pleased with this final collection and that you will enjoy *Little Laureates 2008 North East Scotland* for many years to come.

Contents

Aberlour House Junior School, Elgin

Victor Flavell (11)	1
Keenan Still (10)	2
Kamila Momora (10)	3
Ross Murray (11)	4
Daphne Paget (11)	4
Samantha Harwell (10)	5
Ali McDavitt (10)	5
David Llewellyn (10)	6
Tamsin Matheson (11)	6
Thomas Burge (10)	7
Honor Petrie (10)	7
Amy Parkinson (10)	8
Lorna Brown (10)	9
Robert Rose (10)	10
Mhairi Millward (10)	10
Nicholas Harkess (11)	11
Chloe Sutton (10)	11
Lauren Oram (11)	12
Christopher Pendlebury-Jones (11)	12
George Locke (10)	13

Albyn School, Aberdeen

Donna Gowans (7)	13
Chelsea Wong (7)	14
Alexandra Holden (7)	14
Ellis Watt (7)	15
Heather Baillie (7)	15
Bea Robertson (7)	16
Duncan Depasquale (7)	16
Grace McCrorie (7)	16
Antonia Duncan (7)	17
Elliot Cameron (7)	17
Cameron Reyboz (8)	17
Madeleine Green (9)	18
Manisha Sahota (7)	18
Amelia Ratcliffe-Smith (12)	19
Tariq Pasha (7)	19
Jodie Lawson (7)	20

Ewan Hendry (7)	20
Calvin Park (7)	20
Harris William Salter (7)	21
Adam Auchie (7)	21
Lewis Webster (7)	21
Hannah McMahon (8)	22
Elle Rintoul (7)	22
Patrick Smith (7)	22
Olivia Juett (7)	23
Mhairi Brooker (7)	23
Ngoni Masiyakurima (7)	23
Rebecca Lawrence-Jones (9)	24
Eva Danielle Salter (9)	24
Isaac Ratcliffe-Smith (9)	25
Abbie Wilson (9)	25
Kirsty Taylor (10)	26
Aaron Grayson (9)	26
Eilidh Duthie (10)	27
Abigail Walters (9)	27
Kirstyanne Halliday (9)	28
Jennifer Kelly (8)	28
Rosie Kennedy (8)	28
Eilidh Webster (10)	29
Jamie Richards (9)	29
Georgia Knowles (8)	29
Elizabeth Bell (8)	30
Harry Webster (9)	30
David Wearden (9)	31
Jack McConaghy (9)	31
Jill Russell (11)	32
Lauren Kerr (9)	32
Rosie Malyn (11)	33
Poppy Clayton-Littler (9)	33
Kirsty McNaughton (9)	34
Katherine Buchan (8)	34
Joel Robertson (8)	34
Joyce Chong (10)	35
Holly Reid (9)	35
Molly Minty (9)	35
Thomas Nash (9)	36
Ailsa Duthie (8)	36
Jordan Akram (8)	36

Ngozi Mordi (8)	37
Sophie Milne (9)	37
Ben Sugden (11)	37
Laura Cameron (8)	38
Colette White (8)	38
Peter Haugh (11)	38
Samuel Gilbert (11)	39
Cara McColl (12)	39
Anna Rennie (11)	39
Matthew Macfarlane (12)	40
Caitlin Gainer (11)	40
Laura McDonald (11)	40
Amy Louise Manson (12)	41
Sophie Lawson (8)	41
Emma Davies (12)	41
Paige Payne (11)	42
Tom Falconer (11)	43
Malcolm David Bradley (11)	44
Katrin Obendrauf (11)	45
Bethan Walters (11)	46
Holly Bowden (11)	47
Abbigail Davidson (12)	48
Rhiannon Jones (11)	49
Sandy Richards (11)	50
Samuel Watson (12)	51
Sam Reid (11)	52
Sophie Melville (11)	52
Alice Milne (11)	53
Matthew Carter (11)	53
Ethan James O'Neal (11)	54

Anderson's Primary School, Forres

Madeleine Wright (10)	54
Suzanne Clark (10)	55
Calum Laing (10)	55
Chloe Newlands (10)	56
Elizabeth Bathurst (11)	56
Emma McKay (10)	57
Amy MacDonald (10)	57
Katie Hassan (9)	58
Martin Anderson (9)	58

Connor Barthelmie (10)   59
Lauren Sedgley (10)   59
Josie Sturrock (9)   60
Calum Noel (9)   61
Caitlin O'Neill (10)   62
Joachim Snow (9)   62
Hayley Kenna (10)   63
Ben McCann (9)   63

Chapel of Garioch Primary School, Inverurie

Ewan Winram (10)   63
Christy Donald (10)   64
Ryan Geddes (11)   64
James Hogg (11)   65
Alexander White (11)   65
Annabelle Whipps (11)   66
Gaby Cortés (10)   66
Kirsty Smith (10)   67
Hannah Dobby (11)   67
Shannan Esson (11)   68
Tanya Gill (10)   68
Ashley Dewhurst (10)   68
Beth Strachan (10)   69

Forehill Primary School, Aberdeen

Calum Diack (12)   69
Lesley Jamieson (11)   69
Matthew Brown (11)   70
Glen Ainslie (11)   70
Lee Alexander Forbes (12)   70
Elle Christie (11)   71
Jamie Potts (11)   71
Serena Rae (12)   71
Kara Adamson   72
Louise Clark (11)   72
Steven Clark (11)   73
Kieran Moore (11)   73
Stewart Milne (11)   73
Gemma Rickaby (11)   74
Jake Clayton (11)   74
David McKinlay (11)   75

Shaun Urquhart	75
Stephen Duguid (11)	75
Scott Sim (12)	75

Fraserburgh South Park School, Fraserburgh

James Masson (9)	76
Aaren Cooper (10)	76
Fiona Bruce (9)	76
Jade Kay (9)	77
Luke Maitland (9)	77
Ian Neilson (9)	77
Katie Armstrong (9)	78
Stephen Park (9)	78
Jackie Adams (9)	78
Andrew John Summers (10)	79
Daniel Ross (10)	79
Marc Summers (10)	79
Mark Tait (9)	79

Glenlivet Primary School, Ballindalloch

Ythan Johnson (10)	80
Daniel Balfour (10)	80
Emily West (10)	81
Millie Clethero (8)	82
Forest Lawson (11)	82
Campbell Adamson (8)	83
Katie Durno (8)	83
Lucinda Lock (9)	84
Miles Thomas (10)	85
Lauren McHardy (9)	86
Emma Durno (10)	86
Luke Middleton (8)	87

Grantown Primary School, Grantown-on-Spey

Callum Robert Stewart (11)	87
Roy Gibson (11)	88
Jessica Hart (11)	88
Callum Cockman (11)	89
Andrew Cooke (11)	89
Kate Masson (11)	90
Scott Rose (11)	90

Alan Scott (11)	91
Harry Craig (11)	91
Yandra Banks Brown (11)	92
Brighde Atkinson (9)	92
Holly Dunbar (11)	93
Charlotte McKee (9)	93
Amber Hunter (11)	94
Kristin Currie-Jones (11)	94
Ben Fitzhugh (11)	95
Tom Strang (11)	95
Lauren Simpson (11)	96
Alex Whiller (8)	96
Jason Gordon (11)	97
Jordan O'Donnell (9)	97
Mate Szinyeri (11)	98
Eilidh Sutherland (11)	98
Sonas Walker (11)	99
Shaun Grant (10)	99
Leanne Grant (9)	100
Heidi Dickson (11)	100
Cari Palomino (8)	100
Ashley Emma Rose (10)	101
Darren Gilfillan (10)	101
Annabelle Fraser (9)	101
Caitie Fitzhugh (9)	102
Ross Wilson (8)	102
Hannah Sinclair (10)	102
Joe Dunbar (9)	103
Clay Chisholm (9)	103
Andrew John Stewart (9)	103
Sam Cockman (9)	104
Jack Tulloch (9)	104
Ben Allan (9)	105

Hatton (Cruden) Primary School, Peterhead

Morgan Potter (12)	105
Olivia Paddock (10)	106
Luke Radford (10)	106
Kirsty Clark (10)	107
Callum Duncan (11)	107
Sarah Dignan (10)	108

Beth Stevenson (11)	109
Lauren Kyle (11)	110
Calum Murray (10)	111
Dean Mcleod (12)	111
Sean Buchan (11)	112
Craig Paterson (11)	112
Grant Jamieson (12)	113
Grant Anderson (10)	114
Megan Cantlay (11)	115
Daniel Cantlay (11)	116
Amanda Finnie (11)	117
Rachel Lees (11)	118
Ellis Swainston (11)	119
Gillian Porter (11)	120

Hatton (Fintray) Primary School, Aberdeen
Rees Donaldson (8)	120
Phoebe Hone (9)	121
Rebecca Johnston Harman (7)	121
Bruce Grant (8)	122

Kennethmont Primary School, Huntly
Angus MacLean (11)	122
Morgan McCallum (11)	123
Kyle Florence (11)	123
Cara Simpson (11)	124
Alex Jones (9)	124
Jayne Duthie (9)	125
Beth MacLean (9)	125
Esther Smith (9)	126
Rebecca Henderson (9)	126
Daniel Coursey (10)	127
Becky Jones (11)	127

Luthermuir Primary School, Laurencekirk
Harry Souttar (9)	128
Abbie Farquhar (8)	128
Melissa Rodda (8)	128
Caera Grewar (9)	129
Sean Duncan (8)	129

Alexandra Grace Eavers (9)   129
Calum McGuigan (9)   130
Samuel McGuigan (9)   130

Maud Primary School, Peterhead

Hattie Sherlock (9)   130
Aimee Louise Mowat (9)   131
Ainsley Morrison (10)   132
Ellie Moore (9)   133
Alana Kerry Wallace (10)   133
Lisa Jane Mowat (10)   134
Lauren Smith (10)   134
Connor Matthews (10)   134
Stephanie-Louise Wilson (9)   135
Isla Baxter (9)   135
James Gordon Scott (9)   135
Rebecca Phelan (10)   136

Middlefield Primary School, Aberdeen

Koray Erdogdu (8)   137
Ryan Black (9)   137
Caitlyn Stewart (9)   137
Shannon McPake (8)   138
Aaron Masson (8)   138
Filip Lendzion (10)   138
Rebecca Lowe (11)   139
Jodie Hughes (9)   139
Jack Thomson (9)   139
John Donald (11)   140
Damien Genocchio (11)   140
Conor Brand (11)   140
Dean Barnes (11)   141
Stephen Fraser (11)   142
Connor O'Grady (12)   142
Greg Shearer (11)   142
Rianne Gorman (9)   143
Connor McLeod (8)   143
Tafi Gaza (9)   143
Kamil Szynlklewski (9)   144

Newhills Primary School, Aberdeen

Emily Russell (8)	144
Emma Morrison (8)	144
Chloe Whyte (8)	145
Erin Duncan (8)	145
Rebecca Frew (8)	145
Holly Martin (8)	146
Lewis Hutchison (8)	146
Morgan Stephen (8)	146
Thomas Davidson (8)	147
Chloe Martin (8)	147
Chloe Smith (8)	147
James McIntosh (9)	148
Lewis Burt (8)	148
Owen Rankine (8)	148

Newtonhill Primary School, Stonehaven

Ruri Dickie (8)	149
Adam Christie (8)	149
Aria Kennedy (8)	150
Adam Scott (8)	150
Connor Munroe (8)	151
Ryan Cruickshank (9)	151
Murray Collie (8)	152
Sorcha Hill (8)	152
Ewan Brown (8)	153
Daisy Smith (8)	153

Strathburn Primary School, Inverurie

Euan Banks (8)	154
Emma McDonald (7)	154
Kyle Taylor (7)	154
David Craig (7)	155
Nykita Penny	155
Megan Brown (7)	155
Ryan Garrett (7)	156
Clare Abel (8)	156
Emily Gray (7)	156
Eilidh Thomson (7)	157
Jade Strachan (7)	157
Rikki Russell (7)	157

Cameron McLennan (7)	158
Paisley Howitt (7)	158
Craig Allan (8)	158
Chloe Niamh Clark (7)	159
Beth Alexander (8)	159
Katie Grant (7)	159
Hollie Douglas (6)	160
Marc Mowat (7)	160
Gary Moir (8)	160
Jgordenna Grant (8)	161

Tarland Primary School, Tarland
Ian Leahy (9)	161

Westhill Primary School, Westhill
James Swan (9) & Alex Vicca (10)	162
Jasmine Foubister (9)	162
Morbheinn Nicol (9)	163
James Mackay (9)	163
David Copeland (9) & James Skinner (10)	164
Andrew Wright (8)	164
Holly Alexander & Rachel Black (10)	165
Kirsty McDonald (8)	165
Claire Bruce & Sam Williams (10)	166
Callum Craig (9)	166
Searlait Thom (8)	167
Lewis Williamson (8)	167
Stuart Wright (8)	167
Gavin Ritchie (9)	168
Sam Steel (8)	168
Alakbar Zeynalzade (9)	168
Shannon Adie & Rachael Ronald (10)	169
Emma Stanley (8)	169
Cameron Macdonald & Raymond Aina (9)	170
Callum Ridley (8)	170
Abbie Houston & Emily Berry (10)	171
Daniel Wood & Ryan Smith (10)	172
Rhys Williams (8)	172
Sam Kelsey & Sam Hibbard (9)	173
Ali Hashemizadeh & Callum Chapman (9)	174
Sally Cuthbertson (8)	175

Rhys Mennie (8)   175
Megan MacDonald (9)   176
Marieke Maliepaard (8)   176
Lewis McPherson   177
Amber Love (8)   177
Daniel Bannerman (8)   178
Daniel Hay (8)   178
Jamie Horgan & Ewan Murphy (9)   179
Sean Reid & Fraser Middleton (10)   180
Melanie Alexander (8)   180

The Poems

Everything French Is The Best

France is the best
France, the most popular
Zidance is the best
France should win the Six Nations Rugby Cup
Because Chabal is the best
France beat Scotland and Ireland at rugby
France has got the best Eiffel Tower
Frenchy is my nickname
France is victorious
That is why my name is Victor
French is the best language
It is why my school's motto is
'Plus est en vous'
French men like the frogs
France is cheesy
Cheese is the best
France is the creator of Europe
French crepes are the best in the whole wide world
French toast and pain au chocolat is so good
Same as croissant
Alps are the coolest mountains
Frogs' legs are so good
French rugby and football have got 'Le Coq Sportif'
French is spoken all around the world
The baguettes are good as well
The movie Ratatouille is set in France
Paris has got good shopping
Paris is the best
French fries are definitely the best
Weather is beautiful in France
Concorde is the fastest plane ever and it is French
France is just the best!

Victor Flavell (11)
Aberlour House Junior School, Elgin

Chickens

I have twelve chickens
Six are black and six are brown
They aren't a pain
Chickens run up and down.

Chickens squawk all day long
Chickens waddle weirdly

Some chickens fly up, up into the sky
They scratch around for things
They don't fly up very high
Because we clipped their wings.

Chicken squawk all day long
Chickens waddle weirdly.

Chickens like to eat lots of food
They like to eat carrots
Lettuce and veggies
They eat it when they are in a good mood.

Chickens squawk all day long
Chickens waddle weirdly.

Chickens are cool you should get some
But in the evening they like to go to bed.

Chickens squawk all day long
Chickens waddle weirdly.

Keenan Still (10)
Aberlour House Junior School, Elgin

Shopping

Shopping, shopping, it's such fun,
Shopping's made for everyone!

We love going shopping,
Near or far,
We sometimes need to buy
Some knickers or a bra.

Shopping, shopping, it's such fun,
Shopping's made for everyone!

I want to buy some make-up
I know, some lipgloss,
But I'll use Rimmel
Because I want to look like Kate Moss.

Shopping, shopping, it's such fun,
Shopping's made for everyone.

At the shoe shop I will buy
Some comfortable shoes, I need some.
I put them on and have a try
I love those ones, I'll take them.

Shopping, shopping, it's such fun,
Shopping's made for everyone!

Now we're going to the restaurant
We're starving, don't you know.
We've finished our food and chatted a lot
And now we're about to go.

Shopping, shopping, it's such fun
Shopping's made for everyone!

Kamila Momora (10)
Aberlour House Junior School, Elgin

My Family

My brother is sixteen and he is cool
He likes to play in the swimming pool.
Dominic is his name, he is very tall
He is very good at football.

My sister is from Asia
And she likes going to Malaysia.
Eleanor is her name, she is very pretty,
She thinks I am very witty.

My mum and dad do not like the cold
And they are not old.
George and Edel are their names
And they live in India.

And then there is me, Ross,
I like to be the boss.
I am eleven years old
And I am as good as gold!

Ross Murray (11)
Aberlour House Junior School, Elgin

My School

You should see my school,
The children are mad.
They push the teachers in the pool,
The teachers constantly say we are bad.

In the classroom it is radical man,
The teachers hanging from the ceiling,
Being hit on the head with a pan
To try and give them some feeling.

We say we are kind and caring,
But teachers just say we are freaky.
We are the most daring
And the kings of being cheeky.

Daphne Paget (11)
Aberlour House Junior School, Elgin

My Week

On Monday I feel marvellous on the first day of the week
On Tuesday I feel cheeky 'cause I gave my mum cheek
On Wednesday I feel wonderful, a quiet day at school
On Thursday I feel thoughtful as I walk through the pool
On Friday I feel frightened as it's spelling test day
On Saturday I feel sleepy and too tired to go and play
On Sunday I feel sad as I'm going back to school tomorrow!

Samantha Harwell (10)
Aberlour House Junior School, Elgin

Monsters

If you wake up in the night
And you get a fright,
You have probably seen a monster!
It will have claws
Not cat paws
And will probably have big teeth.

They're fat and hairy,
The opposite of a fairy.
You can smell its breath when it laughs
It obviously needs a bath!
They have horns,
As sharp as thorns,
That stick right out of its nose.

When you scream
It likes to leave
And go back to its home.
It curls up in bed
Cuddles its teddy
And then just starts to cry.
It never gets any friends!

Ali McDavitt (10)
Aberlour House Junior School, Elgin

My School

In school, life everywhere,
Learning all the things for life
And teachers say they care
But we always land in strife.

Bubbles in the science lab
Snoring in the English room
PE getting rid of the flab
And making the teachers fume.

Being evil to the teachers
We have to do what we're told
It's like they're annoying preachers
Plus they're always old.

Are you a little teacher's pet?
Are you an evil little boy?
Do you always forget
Or are you just being coy?

One last thing, you'll feel the heat
When you've gone to see the head
Waiting, scared, on dreaded seat,
There's no point because you'll soon be dead!

David Llewellyn (10)
Aberlour House Junior School, Elgin

The Sky

Stars in the sky with a blink of an eye
Shining brightly in the dark blue sky.

Mercury and Jupiter, Pluto and Mars
Sweets and sugar but I especially love Mars bars.

Looking back to the story, the man on the moon,
Picking up evidence with a spoon.

When the morning comes and the sun rises
People usually get lots of surprises.

Tamsin Matheson (11)
Aberlour House Junior School, Elgin

My Dad

My dad's awesome
He's totally cool.
We have fun in the garden
And we play football.

My dad's fantastic
He's totally wicked.
We always have fun
Playing a good game of cricket.

My dad's so wonderful,
He's totally funny.
We have fun in the winter
Sledging on his big tummy.

My dad's so weird,
He's totally mad.
He's wacky and wonderful,
But hey, that's my dad!

Thomas Burge (10)
Aberlour House Junior School, Elgin

Feelings

Friendship gets you through things
But sometimes gets you down.

Partnership makes you happy
But some people will make you frown.

Love is pretty
But it will make some people mad.

Evil feels good
But really it is bad.

But best of all
Happiness
Is always the best.

Honor Petrie (10)
Aberlour House Junior School, Elgin

The 6M Team

There is Chloe
Smart and great
She's a person no one could hate.

There is Ross
He never gets cross
And is fab at sport.

There is Emma
Who's there if you need a laugh
Her dad's a member of staff.

There is Rory
Who isn't gory
He likes small chairs.

There is Keenan
He likes to run
And enjoys the sun.

There is Mhairi
Who likes the safari
She loves art.

There is Sammy
Who plays the violin
She's always smilin'.

There is Tamsin
Who's quite good at runnin'
She's in my dorm too.

There is Victor
He is from France
And not afraid to dance.

There is Kamila
She likes vanilla
Who's also in my dorm.

There is Honor,
She likes sweets
And never cheats.

There is Ali
Who's always happy
He has a sister too.

Mr Mutton
He's our teacher
And he calls us a team.

Then there is me
My name's Amy
And sisters I have three.

Amy Parkinson (10)
Aberlour House Junior School, Elgin

Brothers

Why have brothers?
They annoy their mothers,
They make such a racket
And pop all the crisp packets.

They annoy the cat,
They make sounds like rats,
They are always bad,
They make their dads mad.

They never clean up,
They always say sup,
They play with their food,
They are always in a grumpy mood.

Why have brothers?
They annoy their mothers,
They are such a pest,
I wish they would give it a rest!

That's what brothers are like!

Lorna Brown (10)
Aberlour House Junior School, Elgin

My Puppy

My puppy,
He is really scruffy
When he comes out of the bath he is fluffy.

My puppy,
Koda he's called,
He likes to chase my cricket ball.

My puppy,
My puppy is brown,
When you take his ball he likes to frown.

My puppy
Koda has very long ears
We have fun in all the years.

Robert Rose (10)
Aberlour House Junior School, Elgin

Seasons

Spring, spring, spring,
Lambs jumping up and down
Daffodils and tulips here and there.

Summer, summer, summer,
Long sunny days
Lots of ice creams every day.

Autumn, autumn, autumn,
Brown, green, red, golden and orange,
Leaves falling everywhere.

Winter, winter, winter,
Wrapped up warm
Sitting by the fire.

Mhairi Millward (10)
Aberlour House Junior School, Elgin

Summer

Summer is when it's hot and nice,
That's summer.
Summer is when ice cream melts and when people go to the beach,
That's summer.
Summer is when children play cricket and have summer holidays,
That's summer.
Summer is when all the animals come out of the caves,
That's summer.
Summer is when the sky is light-blue and water is warm,
That's summer.

Nicholas Harkess (11)
Aberlour House Junior School, Elgin

The Season

First of all there's spring
At the beginning of the New Year
The birds start to sing
That's something that everyone seems to hear.

Summer comes after
Most people go on holiday
There's always lots of laughter
As you fly away.

It's autumn now
Bonfire night is next
Look at the fireworks, *wow!*
We all give a cheer.

Winter is last
Soon school will start
It goes so fast
Sit and think, time to be smart!

Chloe Sutton (10)
Aberlour House Junior School, Elgin

Candyland

When I close my eyes at night
I catch a plane and fly
Through misty clouds of candyfloss
That stream across the sky.

My destination's Candyland
A world of tasty treats,
With gummy bears and lollypops
And all my favourite sweets.

Rivers flow with chocolate
Warm, lovely and smooth,
Reeds are made of laces,
That shimmer when they move.

Houses made of gingerbread
With liquorice on the floor
Have lollipops for windows
And Poppets for a door.

When morning comes I have to leave
It's time to rise and shine,
It's a shame to leave my Candyland
I was having a yummy time.

Lauren Oram (11)
Aberlour House Junior School, Elgin

The Box Man

There once was a man in a box
Who was dreaming of eating a fox.
He looked up in the night
Having a fright
To find he was eating his socks!

Christopher Pendlebury-Jones (11)
Aberlour House Junior School, Elgin

Scotland

Scotland is the best
Most of the islands are in the west
They make Irn-Bru
And different whiskies too
Scotland is the best.

They often play the pipes
The flag has two white stripes
It's always cold with lots of ice
But eating haggis is really nice,
Scotland is the best.

George Locke (10)
Aberlour House Junior School, Elgin

Weather, Weather, Weather

Weather, weather, weather,
I don't like lightning,
Nor do I like thunder,

Especially I don't like them together!
I would hide under the bed.

Weather, weather, weather,
I love the sun,
Who likes the rain?
I don't.

Weather, weather, weather,
I like the snow,
You can make a snowman and ski around.
Who likes the weather?
I do!
Me too!

Donna Gowans (7)
Albyn School, Aberdeen

Weather, Weather

The sun is very hot like a burning pan.
I wish I had shade from a perfect fan
Weather, weather, weather, weather.

I don't like the snow because it is cold in the streets,
Girls and boys go out to play in their gardens every day,
Weather, weather, weather, weather.

It splashes and splashes in the shower of rain
Like a puddle in the windowpane.
Weather, weather, weather, weather.

The fog is like a blow of your mouth
Windy, swirly like a tornado in the town
Weather, weather, weather, weather.

Chelsea Wong (7)
Albyn School, Aberdeen

Weather

Weather, weather, weather,
Pitter-patter, it's the rain against the windowpane.
Weather, weather, weather,
That sun is boiling my back and it's fun to play in.
Weather, weather, weather,
It's white outside, you can build a snowman.
Weather, weather, weather,
Bing, bang, bong, it's the lightning!
Weather, weather, weather,
Do you like the weather?

Alexandra Holden (7)
Albyn School, Aberdeen

Lovely Weather

S now is wonderful
N ow it's time for birds and hedgehogs to hibernate
O wls and polar bears like snow
W inter is wonderful and the best weather I like

S un is nice
U nder the trees is shade
N ow it is shining
N ow it is time to swim
Y oung people outside

W eather is nice
I cebergs are cold
N oisy fireworks
D rizzling rain on houses

R ainbows are shining
A eroplanes are flying
I cy rivers and oceans
N ice clouds
Y achts are on the sea.

Ellis Watt (7)
Albyn School, Aberdeen

Weather

S un is special, sun is fun
U nder the sun people are sunbathing
N ow it's much hotter we're having a water fight squirting Mum!

R ain is running in my street, my mouse is frightened
A big rainstorm is hitting our house
I like the noise of it hitting the ground
N ow it is forming big puddles outside.

Heather Baillie (7)
Albyn School, Aberdeen

The Splash, Splash Rain

Hear the sound of the rain
On the windowpane
We go out to play
We can splash in puddles all day.

At night I heard a rainstorm
Pick, pack, tick, tack
Pitter-patter, hear the sound.

Jump, jump, jump,
Splash, splash, splash, jump
In the puddles all day long.

Bea Robertson (7)
Albyn School, Aberdeen

Weather

S now is white
N ow the snow is melting
O n the road, there is snow
W hen you go to sleep snow comes from the sky

S ometimes the sun comes out
U nder the clouds there is the sun
N ow the sun hides behind the clouds.

Duncan Depasquale (7)
Albyn School, Aberdeen

Weather

Rain is wet and fun to play in
I like the rain's noise
Now the rain goes pitter-patter *splash!*

Sun, sun, sun is hot and orange
I love the way it shines.

Grace McCrorie (7)
Albyn School, Aberdeen

In The Weather

Weather, weather, weather,
I love the sun, it is always hot
You get to sunbathe in the sun.

Weather, weather, weather,
I hate the rain, it is always cold.
I don't care what people say,
I hate the rain, it is always wet.

Weather, weather, weather,
I love snow it is always fun
To play in it and make snowballs.

Antonia Duncan (7)
Albyn School, Aberdeen

Weather

S now is white and fun to play in
N o one can see the road
O n the ground it is white
W here has all the grass gone?

S un is hot
U nder the sun let's have fun
N o one wants to go home.

Elliot Cameron (7)
Albyn School, Aberdeen

Anger

Anger is red like exploding wires flying in the air.
Anger tastes like red hot chillies on my tongue.
Anger smells like burning steam.
Anger looks like red fire.
Anger feels like you are going to be mad.
Anger reminds me of the war.

Cameron Reyboz (8)
Albyn School, Aberdeen

Hatred

What does it sound like?
Hatred sounds like wind wrapping round your hair
And throwing it about.
What does it taste like?
Hatred tastes like the strong salt of the sea in your mouth.
What does it smell like?
Hatred smells like a bin that has been ripped open by a fox
And chucked on the ground.
What does it look like?
Hatred looks like big green spots covering your eyes.
What does it feel like?
Hatred feels like all of the skin being ripped off your hands.
What colour is it?
Hatred is the colour of ghastly green oozing from a mud hole.
What does it remind me of?
Hatred reminds me of when music is played but I don't want to hear it.

Madeleine Green (9)
Albyn School, Aberdeen

Weather

Weather, weather,
Whatever the weather
It might be sunny
It's hot and lovely to be in.
Sun, sun, sun,
The sun is very hot,
It's like a burning pan,
I love the sun so much.

Weather, weather,
Whatever the weather.
It might be snowy
It's wet, cold and horrible to be in,
Snow, snow, snow.

Manisha Sahota (7)
Albyn School, Aberdeen

The Blackout

Walking in the silence
I could see only shapes,
Far away in the distance
There were torches that shone on my face.

The siren rang
Warning everyone,
I began to sprint,
The silence that once hung had gone.

Suddenly I felt myself falling,
I landed on the rubble.
I couldn't move, I felt shocked,
I was in big trouble!

I scrambled up and started running,
I could hear the screams and shouts.
All the bombs and the whistling,
But worst of all I could hear the building's burning.

The smoky taste that hit my throat
Made me stop and cough,
I ran on and my only thought was
'Wow, Germany is tough!'

Amelia Ratcliffe-Smith (12)
Albyn School, Aberdeen

Weather

Weather, weather, weather,
Rain is wet
You can splash in it
It falls from the sky.

Snow, snow, snow
Cold, cold, cold,
It is always cold,
Snow is freezing.

Tariq Pasha (7)
Albyn School, Aberdeen

Love

Love is pink like love hearts on a valentine's card.
Love smells like perfume in a bottle.
Love looks like a big pink valentine's card shaped into a love heart.
Love tastes like cookies with little hearts on them.
Love sounds like someone singing a beautiful song.
Love feels like my bed when I go to sleep at night.
Love reminds me of my family when they tickle me.

Jodie Lawson (7)
Albyn School, Aberdeen

Happiness

Happiness reminds me of Christmas.
Happiness sounds like children in the park.
Happiness feels like Valentine hearts.
Happiness tastes like ripe plums on a bush.
Happiness is pink like Valentine's Day.
Happiness looks like my new imperial star destroyer.
Happiness smells like fully grown apple blossom.

Ewan Hendry (7)
Albyn School, Aberdeen

Rain, Oh Rain

R ain, oh rain, rain can be good and rain can be bad
A shower, a shower, oh a shower, showers let the plants grow
I like to go outside each day and have fun today
N oisy weather, noisy weather, I hear the rain,
    the rain on the window sill, *splish, splash!*

Calvin Park (7)
Albyn School, Aberdeen

Anger

Anger is brown like an angry mob going to get you.
Anger feels like a sharp pin.
Anger tastes like a wiggling cockroach.
Anger smells like a broken car when you're in a hurry.
Anger looks like your dad beating you at karate.
Anger reminds me of when I broke my best Lego model.
Anger sounds like my family out playing golf without me.

Harris William Salter (7)
Albyn School, Aberdeen

Happiness

Happiness tastes like muffins freshly made.
Happiness is pink like the magnificent sunset over the sea.
Happiness feels like your mum giving you a cuddle.
Happiness sounds like children playing in the playground.
Happiness looks like children opening their presents
                                                on Christmas Day.
Happiness reminds me of my birthday.
Happiness smells like chocolate.

Adam Auchie (7)
Albyn School, Aberdeen

Fear

Fear reminds me of white ghosts at Hallowe'en.
Fear is grey like a rain cloud about to rain.
Fear smells like a fire in the woods.
Fear sounds like the wind rattling the door back and forwards
                                                on a stormy night.
Fear tastes like mushy peas on my plate at teatime.

Lewis Webster (7)
Albyn School, Aberdeen

Laughter

Laughter reminds me of my dad tickling me on the couch
and my dogs jumping up.
Laughter smells like chocolate melting in a pan.
Laugher tastes like pasta in my mouth.
Laughter sounds like children giggling in the park.
Laughter feels like scrambled eggs on toast.
Laughter is pink like pigs in a pen.
Laughter looks like people pulling funny faces at me.

Hannah McMahon (8)
Albyn School, Aberdeen

Love

Love is red like a rose.
Love looks like a love heart on Valentine's Day.
Love tastes like valentine hearts.
Love reminds me of sending valentine's cards.
Love smells of chocolate cake cooking in the oven.
Love feels like a soft blanket with love hearts on it at night.
Love sounds like a beautiful song at night.

Elle Rintoul (7)
Albyn School, Aberdeen

Fun

Fun reminds me of when I fell out of the tree last summer.
Fun looks like children playing in the park.
Fun tastes like marshmallows around the camp fire.
Fun smells like a bar of chocolate waiting to be sold.
Fun is blue like a blue skateboard glistening in the sun.
Fun sounds like a go-kart whizzing down a hill.
Fun is orange like a tiger having fun.

Patrick Smith (7)
Albyn School, Aberdeen

Fun

Fun is lilac like balloons at my birthday party.
Fun looks like animals roaming in an open space.
Fun feels like a big chocolate cake ready to be eaten.
Fun sounds like children playing with a new toy.
Fun tastes like a huge chocolate whippy with a Flake.
Fun smells like perfume in a pink bottle.
Fun reminds me of when I go bowling with my mum and dad.

Olivia Juett (7)
Albyn School, Aberdeen

Laughter

Laughter is blue like dolphins in the ocean.
Laughter tastes like salty popcorn.
Laughter sounds like laughing hyenas.
Laughter smells like people having their feet tickled.
Laughter reminds me of when I was ticklish all over.
Laughter looks like pink dolphins in the sea.
Laughter feels like feathers tickling you.

Mhairi Brooker (7)
Albyn School, Aberdeen

Fun

Fun smells like new toys being bought.
Fun tastes like a chocolate being eaten.
Fun looks like I'm tickled by my Mum.
Fun is blue like my Nintendo GameCube.
Fun sounds like a rock star being in a concert.
Fun reminds me of going to my friend's house.
Fun feels exciting with a lot of activities.

Ngoni Masiyakurima (7)
Albyn School, Aberdeen

My Favourite Feeling Is Happiness

What sound is it?
Happiness sounds like lovely music.
What taste is it?
Happiness tastes like caramel chocolate.
What smell is it?
Happiness smells like fresh air on a summer day.
What look is it?
Happiness looks like me pulling off wrapping paper.
What does it feel like?
Happiness feels like a soft breeze in the air.
What it reminds me of.
Happiness reminds me of being in a very happy family.

Rebecca Lawrence-Jones (9)
Albyn School, Aberdeen

Love

What does it sound like?
Love sounds like birds singing in the tree tops.
What does it taste like?
Love tastes like thick sweet chocolates.
What does it smell like?
Love smells like lavender with roses blooming.
What does it look like?
Love looks like a heart looking beautiful.
What does it feel like?
Love feels like a teddy bear giving you a hug.
What does it remind you of?
Love reminds you of your family.
What colour is it?
Love is a scarlet colour like a ruby.

Eva Danielle Salter (9)
Albyn School, Aberdeen

Anger

What sound is it?
Anger sounds like a devil laughing.
Anger sounds like thunder crashing in the night.
What taste is it?
Anger tastes sour like a bitter and sharp lemon.
What smell is it?
Anger smells dusty like an old dungeon.
What look is it?
Anger looks like a very hot volcano erupting and destroying everything.
What feel is it?
Anger feels like a drum pounding in my head.
What it reminds me of.
Anger reminds me of my sister teasing me by hiding my things
And messing up my room.

Isaac Ratcliffe-Smith (9)
Albyn School, Aberdeen

Anger

What does it sound like?
Anger sounds like lots of people shouting in a fight.
What does it taste like?
Anger tastes like hot chillies burning in your mouth.
What does it look like?
Anger looks like smoke coming out of someone's ears.
What does it feel like?
Anger feels like you want to hit someone.
What does it remind me of.
Anger reminds me of getting shouted at by my dad.
What colour is it?
Anger is as red as tomato ketchup getting ready for a chip to get
dipped into it.

Abbie Wilson (9)
Albyn School, Aberdeen

Happiness

What does it sound like?
Happiness sounds like people singing in the choir.
What taste is it?
Happiness tastes like Lindt milk chocolate.
What smell is it?
Happiness smells like extremely cool fresh air.
What look is it?
Happiness looks like beautiful red roses in the garden.
What feel is it?
Happiness feels like icing on a birthday cake.
What it reminds me of.
Happiness reminds me of my birthday when I eat the cake
And open all my presents.

Kirsty Taylor (10)
Albyn School, Aberdeen

Anger

What does it sound like?
Anger sounds like a kettle boiling and whistling.
Anger sounds like waves crashing against the rocks.
What does it taste like?
Anger tastes like a bitter lemon.
What does it smell like?
Anger smells like our smelly washing basket.
What does it look like?
Anger looks like the devil's tummy.
What it reminds me of.
Anger reminds me of getting injured in a football match.

Aaron Grayson (9)
Albyn School, Aberdeen

Happiness Is Great

What sound is it?
The sound of happiness is me on my bike riding in the rain
of the March days.
What taste is it?
The taste of happiness is a big wedding cake being cut ready
to be gobbled down.
What smell is it?
The smell of happiness is a big bunch of lovely roses fresh
from the florist.
What look is it?
The look of happiness is a birthday party with lots of screaming
and squealing children.
What does it feel like?
The feel of happiness is touching a balloon at a joyful birthday party.
What it reminds me of.
Happiness reminds me of my family for they are loving and caring.

Eilidh Duthie (10)
Albyn School, Aberdeen

Fear

What does it sound like?
Fear sounds like a drum pounding helplessly in my head
As I try to sleep in my soft silky bed.
What does it feel like?
Fear feels like every happy feeling has disappeared from the world
As you stand being bullied because your hair is curled.
What does it smell like?
Fear smells like horrible Brussels sprouts cooked in the heat
As well as all those yucky things that children hate to eat.
What does it remind me of?
Fear reminds me of the sounds I hear at night
As you hear the door creak you get such a fright.

Abigail Walters (9)
Albyn School, Aberdeen

Fear

What sound is it?
Fear sounds like a creaking noise in my bedroom.
Fear sounds like my mum and dad shouting at each other.
Fear sounds like thunder and lightning crashing through the night.
Fear sounds like the wind howling in the black sky.

What it reminds me of?
Fear reminds me of when I was on a huge diving board.
Fear reminds me of when I was watching Doctor Who.
Fear reminds me of when I got bitten by a baby shark.

Kirstyanne Halliday (9)
Albyn School, Aberdeen

Happiness Is All Around

Happiness is violet like a flower.
Happiness sounds like children laughing.
Happiness tastes like sweet sugar.
Happiness smells like flowers in a garden.
Happiness looks like a heart floating in the sky.
Happiness feels like fluffy cotton wool.
Happiness reminds me of my bunny having babies.

Jennifer Kelly (8)
Albyn School, Aberdeen

The Feeling Of Sadness

Sadness is blue, the colour of someone's tears.
It sounds like a newborn baby's cry.
It tastes like a plate of food with no flavour.
It smells of mouldy bitter cheese.
It looks like a flower dying.
It feels like you have lost something special.
It reminds me of my grandad.

Rosie Kennedy (8)
Albyn School, Aberdeen

Silence

Silence is the pale pink colour of a half-open rose bud.
Silence is the sound of an empty room.
Silence tastes like the soft and fluffy cream in a delicious cake.
Silence smells like the sweetest flowery perfume.
Silence looks like a peaceful summer garden in full bloom.
Silence feels like a silky cloud.
Silence reminds me of waking up in the middle of the night.
Without silence, life would be an absolutely deafening place to be.

Eilidh Webster (10)
Albyn School, Aberdeen

The Warm Touch Of Happiness

Happiness is yellow like the sun shining in the midday sky.
It sounds like a mighty lion roaring.
It tastes like a delicious cake fresh from the oven.
It smells like a sunflower swaying in the wind.
It looks like the man in the moon beaming down on us.
It feels like a ball of light shining in my hands.
Happiness reminds me of the summer sun gleaming
in the clear blue sky.

Jamie Richards (9)
Albyn School, Aberdeen

Anger

The colour of anger is red like a fierce exploding volcano.
It sounds like the thunder of enormous drums going louder and louder.
It tastes like hot chilli peppers burning your tongue to pieces.
It smells like smoke coming out of my mouth.
It looks like a bull with huge horns coming right at you.
It feels like something's putting their claws into you.

Georgia Knowles (8)
Albyn School, Aberdeen

Anger

What anger sounds like.
Anger sounds like roars of thunder crashing in the night.
Anger sounds like lots of people stamping up the stairs.
Anger sounds like waves crashing the rocks.

What anger tastes like.
Anger tastes like lemon being squeezed into your mouth.

What anger looks like.
Anger looks like a bull about to charge.

What anger feels like.
Anger feels like a big hot flame rising inside you.
Anger feels like a raging devil.

What anger reminds me of.
Anger reminds me of being sent to my room.

Elizabeth Bell (8)
Albyn School, Aberdeen

Anger

What sound is it?
Anger sounds like somebody screaming in the night.
What taste is it?
Anger tastes like a bitter lemon that's really old.
What smell is it?
Anger smells like muddy stuff in the water.
What look is it?
Anger looks like angry faces.
What feel is it?
Anger feels like when I pull my sister's hair.
What it reminds me of.
Anger reminds me of when my friend pushed me off my trampoline
And after I was very angry.

Harry Webster (9)
Albyn School, Aberdeen

Hatred

What sound is it?
Hatred sounds like someone with a whip whipping the ground.
What taste is it?
Hatred tastes like blood dripping down your arm.
What smell is it?
Hatred smells like a fiery furnace.
What does it look like?
Hatred looks like dark red.
What does it feel like?
Hatred feels like a scary nightmare.
What it reminds me of.
Hatred reminds me of my cousin knocking down my models.

David Wearden (9)
Albyn School, Aberdeen

Hate

What sound is it?
Hate sounds like thunder destroying the sky.
What taste is it?
Hate tastes like time.
What smell is it?
Hate smells like poo!
What look is it
Hate looks like a monster.
What feel is it?
Hate feels like being punched.
What it reminds me of.
Hate reminds me of an explosion.

Jack McConaghy (9)
Albyn School, Aberdeen

Fear

Fear sounds like a deadly scream followed by an awkward silence.
Fear is the colour black for all the people walking alone in the darkness
Waiting for something to happen.
Fear tastes like cheese; sometimes it's horrible, sometimes it's lovely
But most of the time it's sweet.
Fear smells like a surgery room when you're not quite sure what's
going to happen next.
Fear looks like a little girl after she watches 'The Grudge'
It just keeps flooding back in your memory.
Fear feels like when you're home alone and you hear a creak
on the stairs
And you just freeze up and listen for more.
Fear reminds me of all the Point Horror books I've read,
Some of it's exciting, some of it's freaky
And some of it's thrilling and it just makes you want to read more.

Jill Russell (11)
Albyn School, Aberdeen

Anger

What sound is it?
Anger sounds like a sea crashing in a storm at midnight.
Anger sounds like a bullet racing through the woods to an animal.
Anger sounds like a whistling kettle boiling and getting louder
and louder.
What it reminds me of.
Anger reminds me of my sister annoying me by spoiling my games.
What taste is it?
Anger tastes like a sour lemon in your mouth on a winter's day.
What colour is it?
Anger is the colour of red like blood dripping from a fresh cut.

Lauren Kerr (9)
Albyn School, Aberdeen

The Blackout

I'm out in the blackout not knowing where I am
I listen to the people as quickly as I can
Hearing screaming voices as I run up and down the ramp.
I can see faint shadows running frantically around
Not knowing what's going to happen to the people around town.
The sirens are twitching time to time, I get this funny feeling
                                                    that I might cry.

I feel scared, time after time,
My parents are always worried what would happen to me
                                        in the blackout.
I need to run inside, safe and warm where I can cosy up by
                                        the roaring fire
Play snakes and ladders, get into bed and snuggle down
                        and the next day it will all be over.

Rosie Malyn (11)
Albyn School, Aberdeen

Happiness

What does it taste like?
Happiness tastes like chocolate in your tummy.
What does it smell like?
Happiness smells like a new pack of cards ready to play rummy.
What does it look like?
Happiness looks like the sun setting.
What does it feel like?
Happiness feels like you won something worth getting.
What does it sound like?
Happiness sounds like a newborn baby crying.
What does it remind me of?
Happiness reminds me of someone flying.

Poppy Clayton-Littler (9)
Albyn School, Aberdeen

Love

What taste is it?
Love tastes like chocolate melting in our mouth.
What smell is it?
Love smells like roses from my cousin.
What look is it?
Love looks like shining new shoes shimmering in the dark.
What feel is it?
Love feels like a cat's soft fur.

Kirsty McNaughton (9)
Albyn School, Aberdeen

Happiness

Happiness is light pink, as light as a flamingo.
It sounds like rivers flowing with laughter.
It tastes like soft red apples floating in the air.
It smells like the sweetness of chocolate.
It looks like flowers popping in rose bushes.
It feels like I'm floating in mid air.
Happiness reminds me of playing in a huge garden.

Katherine Buchan (8)
Albyn School, Aberdeen

My Anger

Anger is red like a gigantic fierce dragon.
It sounds like an evil person murdering a lost boy.
It tastes like a white-hot chilli burning your tongue.
It smells like a devil swooping past you and picking you up.
It feels like you have exploded right out of a volcano.
Anger reminds me of a bull charging straight at me.

Joel Robertson (8)
Albyn School, Aberdeen

Happiness

What sound is it?
It sounds like the deep ocean.
What taste is it?
It tastes like chocolate melting in your stomach rumbling.
What smell is it?
It smells like fresh buttercups.
What look is it?
It looks shiny as crystal clear.
What it reminds me of.
It reminds me of my birthday and eating my birthday cake
that my sister made.

Joyce Chong (10)
Albyn School, Aberdeen

When I'm Angry!

Anger is the colour red like a volcano erupting.
The sound is like thunder crunching its way through the sky.
The taste of anger is like a pepper sizzling on a plate.
The smell of anger is like trouble waiting to happen.
Anger looks like fire burning from a building.
When I'm angry I feel like my head is going to explode.
Anger reminds me of past times that I would like to forget.

Holly Reid (9)
Albyn School, Aberdeen

When I'm Lonely

Loneliness is the colour of light peach, I feel lonesome.
Loneliness sounds like wolf howls, it churns inside my body.
Loneliness feels like an orphaned lamb.
Loneliness smells like freezing all over.
Loneliness looks like a freezing puppy shivering outside.
Loneliness reminds me of Suzy dying.

Molly Minty (9)
Albyn School, Aberdeen

Fear

Fear is orange like a burning fire.
It sounds like the crackling of a fire.
It tastes like saliva in my dry throat.
It smells like nothing, my nose is blocked.
It looks like darkness, everywhere there are walls surrounding me,
I am trapped!
It feels like I've been pushed in the fridge and it is really cold.
Fear reminds me of singing to an audience.

Thomas Nash (9)
Albyn School, Aberdeen

Crying With Sadness

Sadness is the colour of blue like the cloudy bluish sky.
It sounds like someone crying.
It tastes like plain water.
Sadness smells like something being burnt.
It looks like a glum face.
It feels like something rough.
Sadness reminds me of my dead hamster.

Ailsa Duthie (8)
Albyn School, Aberdeen

I Hate My Anger

Anger looks like a huge red volcano.
It sounds like crashing thunder.
Anger tastes like the hottest chilli on Earth.
It smells like a gigantic cloud of smoke.
Anger looks like a huge fire ball.
It feels like being imprisoned in a jail.
Anger reminds me of a furious bull charging at me.

Jordan Akram (8)
Albyn School, Aberdeen

Anger, My Emotion

Anger is red as a wild fire in the forest.
Anger sounds like an angry lion raging and roaring through
the savannah.
Anger is bitter sour and hot as spicy chilli.
Anger looks like the Devil himself, trying to fool you that he is good.
Anger smells like choking smoke from a fire.
Anger feels like the buggy and cat-o-nine whip being used
on your hands.
Anger reminds me of what I face today at work and play . . .
I face anger.

Ngozi Mordi (8)
Albyn School, Aberdeen

My Happy Feelings

Happiness is yellow like a bright glowing sun.
It sounds like music, birds singing in the morning.
It tastes like strawberries, the sweet juice slips into your mouth.
It smells like a red rose.
It looks like children having lots of fun splashing in the waving sea.
It feels like you are safe in your cosy bed.
Happiness reminds me of when I met Holly and we were laughing
and laughing.

Sophie Milne (9)
Albyn School, Aberdeen

Fun

Fun tastes like ice cream melting on your tongue.
Fun feels like ten-pin bowling at the funfair.
Fun looks like hot yummy hotdogs with lots of ketchup.
Fun smells like melted pain au chocolat.
Fun sounds like a rock band playing.
Fun reminds me of going to the fairground to eat candyfloss.

Ben Sugden (11)
Albyn School, Aberdeen

Crying And Loneliness

The colour of sadness is blue like the sky.
It sounds like crying babies and lonely children.
It tastes like water pouring into a glass.
It smells like food being burnt on a frying pan.
It looks like a very happy clown face that has been turned upside down
to make it a sad face.
It feels like a very soggy towel that has been dried and has become
really rough.

Sadness reminds me of a pet dying.

Laura Cameron (8)
Albyn School, Aberdeen

A Bone Of Jealousy

Jealousy is the colour of the dark grey sky on a cold frosty morning.
It is the sound of a burst of steam.
It tastes like a bitter cup of salt water trickling down your throat.
It smells like a hot lava river burning in your head.
It looks like a piece of metal being bent in half.
It feels like you are stuck in a hole where no one cares about you.
Jealousy reminds you of being thrown in a cave and there's nothing
to do but feel miserable.

Colette White (8)
Albyn School, Aberdeen

Fear

Fear is death looming in the darkness.
Fear feels like the aftermath of war.
Fear tastes like your final breath creeping out.
Fear is black with eyes peeping out.
Fear tastes like a loved one's voice trailing away.
Fear reminds me of hopes of saving people, horribly in vain.

Peter Haugh (11)
Albyn School, Aberdeen

Hate

Hate feels like knives stabbing in your back.
Hate tastes like blood and rotten fruit.
Hate sounds like smashing bottles and teenagers swearing
                                             in the street.
Hate looks like gravestones and dying plants.
Hate is the colour of fire and dark red broken Love Hearts.
Hate smells like the ash of cigarettes.
Hate reminds me of bombs dropped and death.

Samuel Gilbert (11)
Albyn School, Aberdeen

Love

Love looks like a red rose newly sprung in spring.
It tastes like when you take your first bite of creamy milky chocolate.
It's the colour of all the colours of the beautiful rainbow.
It sounds like the birds singing on a lovely sunny morning.
Love smells like freshly made bread following me wherever I go.
It feels like when bitter winter has ended and playful summer
                                             has finally come again.
Love reminds me of Christmas Day in the morning.

Cara McColl (12)
Albyn School, Aberdeen

Laughter

Laughter looks like children playing games in the playground
                                             on a summer day.
Laughter feels like jumping on a trampoline.
Laughter smells like homemade chilli coming out of the oven.
Laughter tastes like popcorn popping on your tongue.
Laughter sounds like a ping pong ball hitting off the table.
Laughter is the colour of yellow just like the sun in the sky.
Laughter reminds me of opening a fizzy can of Coca Cola.

Anna Rennie (11)
Albyn School, Aberdeen

Anger

Anger tastes like hot chilli burning down your throat.
Anger is red like a fire, raging and spreading.
It sounds like a bomb screeching down to the ground
and suddenly exploding.
It feels like a thousand needles being suddenly pierced into your body.
It smells like the feeling of pepper up your nose.
It looks like terrorism happening with no way to stop it
But most of all it reminds me of mountainous waves in a storm
crashing to and fro.

Matthew Macfarlane (12)
Albyn School, Aberdeen

Love

Love is like two golden hearts beating side by side.
Love sounds like the crashing waves on a cold silent night.
Love tastes like a cold snowflake slowly melting on your tongue.
Love smells like freshly baked pancakes just as you walk
into the room.
Love looks like two tiny babies sleeping together in silence.
Love fills your heart with joy.
Love reminds me of a soft lips gently pressed against my own.

Caitlin Gainer (11)
Albyn School, Aberdeen

Laughter

Laughter is bright pink, always cheering you up and if you look more
closely it makes you want to jump.
Laughter sounds like a baby sweetly gurgling in bed.
Laughter tastes like bubbles fizzing in champagne.
Laugher looks like Christmas Day as the children laugh and play.
Laugher smells like bubblegum popping on your tongue.
Laugher feels like a mother's hug on a cold winter day.
Laugher reminds me of a bad joke but you laugh anyway.

Laura McDonald (11)
Albyn School, Aberdeen

Love

Love is pink with red hearts soaring all around.
It tastes like strawberry flavoured chocolates melting in your mouth.
Love sounds like laughter under the shining moonlight.
It smells like roast turkey on Christmas Day with your
family and friends.
Love looks like my little brother falling asleep in my arms.
It feels like someone else's lips softly touching yours.
Love reminds me of my papa who passed away two years ago.

Amy Louise Manson (12)
Albyn School, Aberdeen

Sadness

Sadness is blue like the sky.
Crying makes me sad.
Sadness smells like burnt toast.
It looks like blue paper with no drawings.
It feels like something so cold.
It reminds me of my dead guinea pig.

Sophie Lawson (8)
Albyn School, Aberdeen

Sadness

Sadness is blue like raindrops hammering the ground.
It is a loss of a voice which once echoed your happiness.
Sadness tastes like sipping a glass of boiling lemon juice.
Sadness is like breathing in the rust of an old bicycle.
Sadness is like looking through a cracked mirror.
Sadness is like hoovering the happiness out of you until you're left
with a blank memory.
Sadness reminds me of walking down a dark deserted
vandalised street.

Emma Davies (12)
Albyn School, Aberdeen

The Holocaust

Sitting in the darkness
The cattle train rumbling by,
The smell of cows and their mess
Is everywhere near I.

I was awoken roughly
Feeling damp and cold,
Thrown from the vehicle toughly
With a pair of pyjamas to hold.

I stood alone in my brand new clothes
Tears running down my face,
I have no friends, no one knows
What it's like to be in this place.

Then came a new girl, Martha Lee,
Tall, thin and pale,
The only person there for me
So strong she never did wail.

Then one day the soldiers came
When I was sick and weak,
From then on nothing was the same,
My life was even more bleak.

For I had to face the fact that I
Soon would be taken away.
I would always remember how my best friend,
Was torn from me that day.

And soon it came my turn to go,
Her hand slipped away,
I just hope she will remember my name
For she looked so overwhelmed with dismay.

I entered the chamber
My clothes torn from my back.
That day Martha and I will remember
As my sight turned from light to black.

Paige Payne (11)
Albyn School, Aberdeen

Air Raid

I'm walking through the street
Holding my mum's hand,
Then the siren goes off
Bombs are going to land.

We're running to the shelter
Fire raging all about,
We're almost at the shelter
Then I hear someone shout.

We're dodging falling bricks
Wow, they are hot!
Look at all the bombs,
Oh there's a lot.

Run, run, run,
We're not going to make it.
A bomb just dropped
What will it hit?

We got in the shelter
A bomb just fell,
The smoke's rising up,
Oh what a smell!

The last bomb has landed
Now there's not a sound,
The air raid must be over
No dead bodies can be found.

I step outside
Silence is all around,
Buildings are down
There's still no sound.

Cars upside down
Fire burning still
I wonder who else
Germany will kill!

Tom Falconer (11)
Albyn School, Aberdeen

The Blackout

I'm walking along the street
There's nothing but darkness
And all along the road is covered
With rubble and ash.

I can hear something in the distance
I don't know what it is
But now it's getting louder
And I'm running, running.

I am looking for the public shelter
But I do not know the way
All the smoke is rising
And it's grabbing at my throat.

And then I heard the shouting.
The screaming
And then I heard the rumble of the German planes
The bombs dropping from overhead.

Everyone is running, I've guessed what it is
The siren now screeching in my ear
I ran round the corner
But I was stopped by the fire.

I was scared and lost
My breath was wheezing
And then I looked up, my eyes opened wide
But it was too late.

Malcolm David Bradley (11)
Albyn School, Aberdeen

The Blackout

The wailing of the sirens
Fills the moonlit sky
And in a flash the lights go out
I hear a stranger cry.

I can only make out shadows
Of people here and there
I'm scared and wish I couldn't hear
The screaming everywhere.

The taste of smoke hits my tongue
As bombs go off nearby
I hear planes overhead
Flying very high.

I can smell dust and ashes
Feel the rubble next to me
I am glad that it's so dark
This, I do not want to see.

Slowly I move on
Pleased that I know the streets so well
I see a house quite close to me
And before my eyes it fell.

The flames are really close to me
And I start to cough
A tear runs down my face
Before I run off.

Katrin Obendrauf (11)
Albyn School, Aberdeen

Evacuation

I'm clinging to my mother
I breathe in her sweet smell,
She hugs me tight and kisses me
I hear the porter's bell.

He takes my leather suitcase
And leads me by the hand,
I climb into the roaring train
And there my mother stands.

She waves goodbye
She turns around,
I cry again but lo,
She hears no child's sound.

So I dry my tears, the train starts up
 I move into meadows green,
And suddenly poking out,
Strange creatures can be seen.

But then the train lurches
The creatures are gone
And then the train stops
We're away from the bombs.

We're hustled and bustled
Into the town square,
Among all my classmates
Faint people stand there.

I get picked by a woman
And we move slowly home,
I'm as tired as ever
My legs feel like stone.

And yet I still worry
About my poor mother,
And my cousins and sisters
And my poor sickly brother.

Still, I go into my room
And climb into bed,
I start nodding off
So I rest my poor head.

And still I remember
That dreadful old day
Even though I'm a grandma
With a back strong as hay.

Bethan Walters (11)
Albyn School, Aberdeen

The Shelter

I'm in my bed all silent
Drifting off to sleep
My bed is warm and cosy
I feel for my teddy
She's here, safe and sound.

There's a big crash outside my window
Mum runs in and pulls me away
She's saying it's a bomb
And my heart goes *boom!*

I ran across the garden
Down to the shelter
I slammed shut the shelter door
The smell is earthy soil.

I can hear the bombs dropping
The fire licking at the lamppost
Quickly, I got into the bed
It's cold and damp
Not like my own.

I wake up in the morning
I've got a pain in my foot
The shelter's all flooded
I want to get out
The feeling is horrible
I don't want the war,
Do you?

Holly Bowden (11)
Albyn School, Aberdeen

The Blackout

Everything is dark, still and quiet,
Free from German bombing riot.
Shadows on the move around the place,
Walking down the street, I can't see a single face.

I can smell the odour of burning ash
Spraying everywhere as buildings smash,
Choking smoke and blistering paint,
The smell is powerful I feel faint.

As the city shakes I've been knocked to the gravel
I lie very still as my heart starts to pound.
I can feel rubble as I stand above the floor,
Thank goodness it's not burning me anymore.

The horrible taste of smoke in the air
Is blinding me, choking me and getting in my hair.
It hits the back of my throat pretty fast
I'm glad I'm nearly home at last.

The screaming of sirens and the pounding of feet,
I can hear whistling doodlebugs from the street.
I know I'm out late; I just want to get home
So down several streets I quickly roam.

I arrive home with my gas mask in hand
It's once again silent as I look around the land.
My house has been bombed from overhead
But my family aren't there, could they be dead?

Abbigail Davidson (12)
Albyn School, Aberdeen

The Bombing

All I could see was shadows
As the sirens screeched and wailed
I went running out the house
While holding my teddy bear looking rather pale.

My mum shouted to get in the shelter
While holding something to eat
Suddenly I heard it, the whistling of a bomb
Then we got inside, it was very wet
And what was more, there was no heat.

I smelt smoke coming from the bombsites
I could hear people calling out
It was terrible to hear the sounds so near
There was a roaring of engines
Soaring high up in the sky.

Then I head another whistle
One which shook the ground
My sister screamed, my doggie howled
I was scared but didn't make a sound.
The dog jumped upon my lap and hid its face in my hands.

Another scream, another shout
They came from everywhere all about
I thought my heart had skipped a beat
I felt another bomb drop as the vibrations went through my feet.

Rhiannon Jones (11)
Albyn School, Aberdeen

The Blackout

I'm walking home
And all I see is destruction
Why are bombs dropped on London?
When will we start the reconstruction?

I'm walking home
And it's getting dark,
The blackout has started
So I'll sprint through the park.

I'm running home
The sirens have started,
I wonder if the Germans will come
And if in this war they can be outsmarted.

I'm dashing home
As fast as I can,
I'm feeling scared,
I'm wondering where the first bombing will slam.

I'm flying home,
I can hear rumbling
Still far off,
Some people running, all of them grumbling.

I've just turned into my street,
As I approached I smelt smoke
And as I ran for my bomb shelter
I began to choke!

I'm picking my way through my ruined house
Heading for the backyard
And safety from the bombs,
I wonder if the way is open or is it barred?

I can smell the peeling pain,
I can smell that metallic smell
That sticks to the back of your throat
I wonder if my shelter will save me from this Hell?

In some places it's dark
In others filled with flames.
I slammed a door and a wall collapsed,
Will Mum give me the blame?

I've made it to the bomb shelter
And I've made it in
The bombs are still falling
But when the door opens I fall in the bin!

Sandy Richards (11)
Albyn School, Aberdeen

The Blackout

The night was dark
Not a sound
The night was still
Nobody moved
The planes were coming
Not for good
People were crying
Not of joy
The taste of smoke
At the back of my throat.

A sense of fear
In the air
A single tear
Runs down my face
A sudden chill
Flows down my spine
A bomb
Falls from the sky
I hear its whine
As it passes by
I smell the smoke
From the deadly flames
I hear a scream
Which dies away
Then the bombing stops
At the break of day.

Samuel Watson (12)
Albyn School, Aberdeen

Trying To Get To The Shelter

Running to the air raid shelter as I hear the siren going off
The only thing in the air is smoke, it made me cough.
Sprinting to the air raid shelter trying to get there fast.
Praying as I'm running and hoping that I'll last.

I saw the flames lighting up the sky
Burning down buildings that were very high.
Seeing my town getting damaged made me want to cry,
Seeing the bombs being dropped made me wonder why.

I've now reached the shelter, all safe and sound,
Hearing all the bombs above me made me frown
Then after that it all went quiet and I couldn't hear a sound.
All my family were safe, not injured or dead,
I wanted that dreadful day to end so I went to my bed.

Sam Reid (11)
Albyn School, Aberdeen

The Blackout

I was close to home, it went silent.
The siren went off, everyone was running home.
I went into my back garden
I had to feel for the door to get into the Anderson shelter.
I put on the lamp, I went down to the bottom, it was flooded!
It was quiet for a moment and then I heard a whistling sound falling.
I heard crying and I tried to go to sleep but I couldn't.
It finished after all, I went outside but all I saw were buildings on fire,
Rubble and people under the rubble, I couldn't stop crying.
It was like a horrible nightmare that I never woke up from.
I don't want it to ever happen again,
It was the worst year in 1939 and the worst month was September.

Sophie Melville (11)
Albyn School, Aberdeen

Sadness

Sadness feels like cold red blood dripping across a statue still body.
Sadness tastes like ice cold lumpy porridge on its way into my mouth.
Sadness sounds like someone weeping but I can't find them
                                        to deliver comfort.
Sadness looks like people speaking to me but my ears won't
                                        let me hear.
Sadness is a baby's blue blanket but with no life inside.
Sadness smells like cigarette smoke racing towards my lungs.
Sadness reminds me of darkness as the rain furiously splashes
                                        the world like a giant crying.

Alice Milne (11)
Albyn School, Aberdeen

The Blackout

I'm in my bed
I'm frightened and scared
Then all at once they stop
I can't hear a thing

It's so dark I can't see anything
Then all of a sudden *bang!*
A bomb had dropped so close I could feel the heat
There are screams everywhere.

I get up and look out of my window
It had dropped at Mrs Rosemary's house
There now was nothing there
Just the remains of the house.

Far in the distance I saw bombs dropping
I was feeling the most scared I ever have
Mum shouted, 'Go to the shelter'
I ran as fast as I could all the way there.

I jumped in and climbed onto my small bed
It was a bit damp and cold
Then Mum and Dad ran in and shut the door
For some reason I felt safe then.

Matthew Carter (11)
Albyn School, Aberdeen

Hunger

Hunger is a dull, dull brown, the colour of a tattered old jacket.
It feels like sharp jagged rocks that a lighthouse cannot save
                                                            ships from.
It sounds like the cries of a starving child crying out for food.
It smells like the strongest desire ever, one even stronger
                                                than someone's love.
It tastes like a star, sparkling and full of energy
But it teases your tongue and stays just out of reach so you can't
                                                            taste it.

It looks like a starving stray dog begging for a bone.
It reminds you of a tramp, broken and forlorn on a street corner.

Ethan James O'Neal (11)
Albyn School, Aberdeen

SOE (Save Our Egg)

Mum's in the kitchen
Dad's in the hall
I'm in shock
'Cause my egg's so tall.

Oh no!
The cracker's on the floor,
My egg's changing colour
And I can do no more.

My sister's on a walk
When I want to talk.
I'll have to send a message
So please come quick!

My egg is drying,
It's an emergency
Not to save our souls
But to save our egg!

Madeleine Wright (10)
Anderson's Primary School, Forres

The Clown That Isn't Funny

My big red nose
My tiny little toes
My big yellow suit
My eyes are so cute.

I'm scared of tights
They are so bright
I'm a clown
And my face is brown.

I have golden hair
Beautiful blue eyes
And little rosy cheeks
And that is me.

Suzanne Clark (10)
Anderson's Primary School, Forres

Animals

Monkeys
Tigers
Parrots
Penguins
Lions
Cheetahs
Vultures
Dogs
Bears
Cats
Horses
Pigs
All the animals in the world, they're all so cool
So many animals in the world, all so wonderful!

Calum Laing (10)
Anderson's Primary School, Forres

Girls

Girls are the best
They get what they want
Make-up, jewellery, fashion and boys
Crop tops, denim shorts
Lemonade in the sun
Sleeping in, sneaking out
That's what girls are all about

Partying all through the night
Sneaking back when it's light
We are the best, better than boys
We can wind them up
And they will get annoyed
Stealing their football
Throwing it in the lake
Then we will say
Oops, my mistake!

Remember this poem that I have told you, tell your brother
But watch out, your mum must not hear you!

Chloe Newlands (10)
Anderson's Primary School, Forres

The Boy Of My Dreams

The boy of my dreams has cute black hair.
The boy of my dreams has light brown skin.
The boy of my dreams is so cute and funny.
The boy of my dreams is popular and cool.
The boy of my dreams loves to run.
The boy of my dreams loves to play bugzy.
The boy of my dreams . . .
The boy of my dreams, I hope soon he will notice me and ask me
to the park.

Elizabeth Bathurst (11)
Anderson's Primary School, Forres

My Dog

My dog is the best
The best of the rest
His fluffy golden fur
Shines like a superstar.

He runs about the garden
Having fun playing fetch
My dog is the best
The best of the rest.

My dog is so cute
He's the best you'd ever want
He loves to run and play
All through the day.

My dog is the best!

Emma McKay (10)
Anderson's Primary School, Forres

Girlz Stuff

Lipstick, mascara
Not to forget my tiara
And eyeshadow
The colour of a meadow.

Shoes and fashion
Will always be my passion
And lots of clothes
The colour of the sea.

Jewels are just so cool
My jewel box is so full
Ideal for a magpie
With a hunting eye.

Amy MacDonald (10)
Anderson's Primary School, Forres

My Dog Has A . . .

My dog has a . . .
Funny bone
Fish bone
Chicken bone
Lamb bone
Squeaky bone
Duck bone
Wet bone
Bird bone
And a bone shaped like a stick.

A . . .
Bouncy ball
Wet ball
Squeaky ball
Meaty ball
And a rubber ball
And the final thing she likes is
Attention!

Katie Hassan (9)
Anderson's Primary School, Forres

Cats In A Mood

Cats, cats, big black cats
Always, always sitting on mats.
Big fat cats, never going to bed when they should
I shouted his name but he just stood,
My cat is always in a mood!
My cat's eyes are very green
So in the dark he can always be seen.

Martin Anderson (9)
Anderson's Primary School, Forres

The Old Cottage

No one returns from the haunted house
It just gobbles them up!
There are goblins in the larder,
They seem to be getting harder.
The zombies are vicious,
They are boisterous and suspicious
Of a new one in their ranks.
The witch gives you spanks
With her wooden spoon,
It reminds me of a certain nanny.
The garden is made of graves
They're even in the paves.
I hope you're not going in
Or you'll be up to your chin
In undead skin. Oh you are?
Nice knowing ya!

Connor Barthelmie (10)
Anderson's Primary School, Forres

The Boy In My Heart

The boy in my heart is truly who I want.
He is like a dripping glistening chocolate fountain,
His eyes are like a crystal pool of blue
And I'm sure he's into me, it has to be true.
He always smiles with his laugh in the air,
It's just so hard not to stare.
Only if he'd realise I am his girl
Finally, it's Valentines Day
Right now this poem's being sent away.

Lauren Sedgley (10)
Anderson's Primary School, Forres

What My Dog Likes

My dog's name is Ben, he is a Collie, I'm sure you've heard of him.

My dog likes balls,
Bouncy balls
Tennis balls
Rubber balls
Bark balls
Round balls
Square balls
Sparkly balls
Bone balls
And balls shaped like mice.

My dog likes bones
Biscuit bones
Rubber bones
Funny bones
Tickle bones
Beef bones
Bouncy bones
Tasty bones
And bones shaped like collars.

My dog likes walks
Long walks
Short walks
Wet walks
Dry walks
Jumpy walks
Short walks
Walks with friends
And long walks down by the riverside.

My dog likes snow
Wet snow
Dry snow
Cold snow
Soft snow
Hard snow
Slushy snow
And icy snow.

Tip, if the snow is white it's alright,
Yellow or green, it's just not clean!

My dog's name is Ben, he is a collie and I'm sure you've heard of him.

Josie Sturrock (9)
Anderson's Primary School, Forres

Myths

One is the Big Foot
Who roams the mountains high
But when his feet are on the ground
His head is in the sky.

Next I come to Nessie
Who lies about the sea
But his teeth are the size of melons
And he's bigger than a tree.

Last there is the griffin
Who soars above the ground
He is a magnificent golden bird
With eyes crystal blue and round.

All these creatures are great
But not like you and me
So if you do see one
Run home or they'll have us for their tea.

Calum Noel (9)
Anderson's Primary School, Forres

The Enchanted Place

The glistening water in oceans so deep
The creatures that lie with coral beneath
The bubbles that float to the surface above
A beautiful bird, maybe a dove.

But down below where the fishes play
There may be a shark so stay away
In and out the seaweed swirls
Are dancing dolphins doing twirls.

A mythical mermaid in coral caves
Swimming around in lots of waves
There are twinkling shells, pebbles and rocks
In this different world there would be lots of shocks.

Lots of fish rule this enchanted place
They have magical looks on their face
They love the bubbles, waves, shells and more
They swim and swim and swim galore.

In this beautiful ocean so deep
There is an enchanted kingdom that lies beneath.

Caitlin O'Neill (10)
Anderson's Primary School, Forres

Tigers

I think tigers are rather nice.
Their coats are striped,
Their eyes are green,
They always seem to be very mean.
Their ears are round,
Their teeth are white,
They roam around the forest at night.
They kill cattle, they shouldn't touch
And no one seems to like them much
But I think tigers are nice.

Joachim Snow (9)
Anderson's Primary School, Forres

Chinny The Chinchilla

Chinny the chinchilla has orange teeth which stick up
from the gums beneath.
Chinny the chinchilla has soft grey fur but Chinny the chinchilla
doesn't purr.
Chinny the chinchilla has a sand bath once a week but it doesn't
come from the beach.
Chinny the chinchilla has little beady eyes but they're not like yours
or mine.
Chinny the chinchilla has small paws with tiny white little claws.

Hayley Kenna (10)
Anderson's Primary School, Forres

The Zoo

Yesterday I went to the weird zoo
This is a list of the animals I saw,
A honky wonky wing wang war squirted water on my head,
A dindyead having a birthday,
A beautiful doddleay singing a lovely song,
Then I went to the gift shop and bought a key ring, with every step
you take it makes a little ping
Now I have to stop there, maybe I'll tell my friend to go but only
for a dare!

Ben McCann (9)
Anderson's Primary School, Forres

Wasps

Wasp, wasp, wasps annoy people like fleas,
Wasps, wasp, wasps sting people.
Wasps, wasp, wasps have a colour of black and yellow,
Wasps, wasp, wasps are as ugly as bumblebees.

Ewan Winram (10)
Chapel of Garioch Primary School, Inverurie

Our School

You might think it's boring
And there's no point in going
But not at our school!

We swing on our chair
And shave the teacher's hair,
We drive them to madness
So they're full of sadness,
Only at our school!

We bite, we scratch, we love to play,
This is the rundown of our day . . .
We swing on the music trolley
And beat up the classroom dolly.

We know it's school
And it's a drool
But this is only at our school.

Christy Donald (10)
Chapel of Garioch Primary School, Inverurie

Olly

Olly's so smart but yet so small,
When she gets no attention
She cheeps and begins to do funny things.
She's like a Spitfire in the sky
Until my dog takes her out
So she wriggles and wriggles
Until she breaks free.
I love Olly, she's a star.

Ryan Geddes (11)
Chapel of Garioch Primary School, Inverurie

Bogey

Bogey, bogeys they are yum
Bogeys, bogeys in my tum.
Bogeys, bogeys in my nose,
Bogeys, bogeys wherever I goes.

Bogeys, bogeys in my ear,
Bogeys, bogeys now they're here.
Bogeys, bogeys in my mouth,
Bogey's bogeys in my house.

Bogeys, bogeys in my eye,
Bogeys, bogeys in a pie.
Bogeys, bogeys on my hand,
Bogeys, bogeys on my land.

Bogeys, bogeys on my nail,
Bogeys, bogeys, in the mail.
Bogeys, bogeys on my foot,
Bogeys, bogeys, have a look.

Bogeys, bogeys in my hair,
Bogeys, bogeys everywhere.
Bogeys, bogeys in a bubble,
Bogeys, bogeys get you in trouble.

Now you give it all you've got
And blow into a tissue all your snot!

James Hogg (11)
Chapel of Garioch Primary School, Inverurie

The Eagle

It flaps its wings without a sound
And rarely ever touches ground.
And when you hear the eagle's cries
You can't resist but turn your eyes.
But then you see it fly away
Don't worry; it'll be back another day.

Alexander White (11)
Chapel of Garioch Primary School, Inverurie

My Puppy Tilly

Tilly scratches and bites
And does nothing right
She chews on her toys so vividly bright
Tilly runs in the garden as if there's a fight.

She barks at my mum when she says something nice
When my parents kiss she growls all night.
She jumps on the cat and starts a fight
My mum puts her out and she cries all night
Until we let her in and put her right.

Don't get me wrong
We all love Tilly
Even if she's naughty 24/7
But we can handle that.

Annabelle Whipps (11)
Chapel of Garioch Primary School, Inverurie

Hamsters

Hamsters are cool,
Hamsters are sweet,
Even if every day
They sleep, sleep, sleep.

Hamsters are great,
Hamsters are ace,
If they were allowed
They could win a race.

Hamsters are cute,
Hamsters are soft,
When their whiskers tickle you
You laugh your head off.

Gaby Cortés (10)
Chapel of Garioch Primary School, Inverurie

The Sun, The Sea And The Sky

The sea is a vast open place
It stretches far out into space
The waves are big, powerful and salty
And they shrink as they reach the shore.

The sky is bright and very blue
It shines as nice as ever
The sky is full of fluffy clouds
That look like candyfloss.

The sun is the colour of an apple, red
Their rays are lovely, they never bring dread.
The sun lights the whole Earth
It helps us like light right from birth.

So thanks for the sun, the sea and the sky
It makes me smile as they pass by.

Kirsty Smith (10)
Chapel of Garioch Primary School, Inverurie

Books

Books are magical
Books are true
I know you'll love them too.

Sometimes true
Sometimes false
They're waiting just for you.

Some adventure
Some horror
Loads of different authors.

Some books good
Some books bad
But really, they're all the same.

Hannah Dobby (11)
Chapel of Garioch Primary School, Inverurie

My Dog Murphy

Murphy, oh Murphy
What a cute dog,
When I look for him
He disappears into the fog
But I don't need to worry
Because he uses his nose
To come back to me.
When people see him
They always go *'Ooh!'*

Shannan Esson (11)
Chapel of Garioch Primary School, Inverurie

My Horse

My horse is brown
And if I could, I would give it a crown.
She's got a long stringy mane
But I would never whip her with a cane!

She has a big black tail
And leaves a horseshoe trail.
My horse is so cute
I would never, ever give her away!

Tanya Gill (10)
Chapel of Garioch Primary School, Inverurie

Stars, Sun And The Moon

Stars shine bright
And come out at night.

The moon is big
Bigger than an oil rig!

The ocean is wide
And it can't hide.

Ashley Dewhurst (10)
Chapel of Garioch Primary School, Inverurie

Stars

Stars like to twinkle in the night
While they shine very bright.
Stars light up the great big sky
They are as pretty as a butterfly.

Stars are like diamonds in outer space
They come out at night and show their face.
Stars are quiet, stars are shy,
They are like angels standing high.

That's why I like stars.

Beth Strachan (10)
Chapel of Garioch Primary School, Inverurie

The Storm Is An Eagle

The storm is an eagle.
Its cries are thunder through the sky then it attacks.
Going down at lightning speed it grabs its prey.
The blood is rain falling, falling.
The eagle is a dark cloud high above the ground looking around.
You know it's there when you hear the noise of wind through its wings.
The storm is an eagle.

Calum Diack (12)
Forehill Primary School, Aberdeen

The Storm Is An Elephant

The storm is an elephant,
Stomping its feet loudly is thunder striking.
The storm is an elephant,
Its trunk spraying out a raindrop falling gracefully to the ground.
The storm is an elephant.
Its tail whipping from side to side, a crackling bolt of lightning striking
in the night.

Lesley Jamieson (11)
Forehill Primary School, Aberdeen

The Storm

The storm is a gorilla
It thunders through the jungle chasing away its predators.
The storm is a gorilla
It cries as one of its troop passes away.
The storm is a gorilla
It spins around in circles playing with his mates.
The storm is a gorilla
It snaps branches as it darts around the jungle.
The storm is a gorilla
It swings on the trees with gale winds in its face.

Matthew Brown (11)
Forehill Primary School, Aberdeen

The Storm Is A Shark

The wind is a shark zipping through the clear blue water.
A cyclone is a shark munching on its prey.
An earthquake is a shark fighting and biting for its protection.
A snowstorm is a shark using its pale white belly to camouflage itself.
A tidal wave is a shark jumping out of the water for a seagull meal.
The storm is a shark, brave, bold, but dangerous.
The storm is a shark.

Glen Ainslie (11)
Forehill Primary School, Aberdeen

The Storm Is A Wolf

The wolf howls the wind in the pitch-black night.
The wolf runs at full speed, the lightning speeding through the night sky
While its feet thunderously hitting the ground, the thunder rumbling
through the night sky.
The wolf stops and then chases its tail, a tornado whipping up
everything in its path.

Lee Alexander Forbes (12)
Forehill Primary School, Aberdeen

The Storm Is An Elephant

The storm is an elephant
Spitting rain rapidly out its long wrinkled trunk in the crazy wind.
The storm is an elephant
His huge feet stomping speedily, thunder has struck.
The storm is an elephant
His short tail swaying quickly, lightning has hit.
The storm is an elephant
The noise of the elephant is the wind blowing wildly in the cloudy sky.

Elle Christie (11)
Forehill Primary School, Aberdeen

The Storm Is A Bear

The storm is a bear roaring like thunder.
The storm is a bear lighting the crack of twigs as it runs
through the woods.
The storm is a bear, the wind howling brave and fierce.
The storm is a bear, the hurricane killing its prey.
The storm is a bear, the rain fishing in a river throwing water about.

Jamie Potts (11)
Forehill Primary School, Aberdeen

The Storm Is A Lion

The storm is a lion
When it roars, it is thunder.
The storm is a lion
When it runs, it is lightning.
The storm is a lion
When its feet are thumping, it is strong rain.
The storm is a lion
When it is angry, it is a tornado.

Serena Rae (12)
Forehill Primary School, Aberdeen

The Storm Is An Elephant

The storm is an elephant
Trumping noises, the wind.

The storm is an elephant
Breaking the branches,
Crashing lightning.

The storm is an elephant
Running with the herd,
Hailstones slamming on the ground.

The storm is an elephant
Stomping with its young,
Thunder roaring in the distance.

The storm is an elephant
Spraying water
Landing flat on the ground,
Rain splashing around.

The storm is an elephant laying down for a calm sleep under the trees
The storm quietly stopping.

Kara Adamson
Forehill Primary School, Aberdeen

The Storm Is A Gorilla

The storm is a gorilla,
Banging on his chest,
Is the thunder roaring in the distance.

The storm is a gorilla,
Swinging on the trees
Is the wind.

His tears when another member of his troop dies,
The rain crashing down on the ground.

The storm is a gorilla,
Running across the scattered twigs
Is lightning crackling in the distance.

Louise Clark (11)
Forehill Primary School, Aberdeen

The Storm

The storm is a monkey
Running rapidly through the grass, it is lightning crashing in the
distance.
The storm is a monkey
Hanging and snapping the branches off the tall trees.
The storm is a mad monkey
Jumping around the bushes with hailstones hitting it.
The storm is a monkey
Munching on its cold food in the snow.

Steven Clark (11)
Forehill Primary School, Aberdeen

A Storm Is A Gorilla

A storm is a gorilla, when it cries it is heavy rain.
A storm is a gorilla, when it bangs its chest it sounds as thunder.
A storm is a gorilla, when it runs fast it is lightning.
A storm is a gorilla, when it's twirling through the trees it's a tornado.
A storm is a gorilla when it roars it is thunder.

Kieran Moore (11)
Forehill Primary School, Aberdeen

The Storm Is A Wolf

The storm is a wolf
Lightning speeding across the sky.

The storm is a wolf
Its growl is the thunder.

The storm is a wolf
A pack running through the forest, an earthquake.

The storm is a wolf
A cyclone chasing its prey.

Stewart Milne (11)
Forehill Primary School, Aberdeen

The Storm Is A White Tiger

The wind is a white tiger
Breathing heavily while sleeping under the damp emerald leaves.
The lightning is a white tiger
Creeping through the jungle, standing on the sharp crisp undergrowth.
The thunder is a white tiger
Roaring aggressively at another male tiger.
The rain is a white tiger
Splashing happily in the jungle river with its cubs to cool down
                                    from the blistering sun.
The blizzard is a white tiger
That claws at its prey that get caught in its path.
The tornado is a white tiger
Calming down after a hard day's work.

Gemma Rickaby (11)
Forehill Primary School, Aberdeen

The Storm Is A Wolf

The storm is a wolf running, cascading deeply through the forest,
The wind, blowing along the woodland paths.
Howling, holding a high note, the wind whistling through a tight gap
                                    in the tree branches.
Zooming swiftly around, dodging hunters.
The wolf is lightning, determinedly striking its prey, snapping
                          the bones, crackling lightning.
Jumping, rising up then landing the rain, heavily pattering
                                    on the ground.

Jake Clayton (11)
Forehill Primary School, Aberdeen

My Kite

My kite is a Rottweiler
His tail wags in the wind.
He barks at the noise of the wind.
He tugs at the lead and if you let him go
He will run and run and run.

David McKinlay (11)
Forehill Primary School, Aberdeen

My Kite Is A Dog

My kite is a German Shepherd.
He wags his tail when he sees his owner.
When he is let off his lead
He runs away to the beach and jumps in the water.

Shaun Urquhart
Forehill Primary School, Aberdeen

My Kite Is A Dog

My kite is my Husky dog.
He wags his tail in a happy way in the wind.
He runs about in the gales until he gets tired
He lays on his bed amongst the clouds fast asleep.

Stephen Duguid (11)
Forehill Primary School, Aberdeen

My Kite Is A Dog

My kite is a dog,
It sniffs the air as it pulls its owner along.
It wags its tail in the wind.

Scott Sim (12)
Forehill Primary School, Aberdeen

Anger

The colour of anger is deep red blood spewing out a sick, sick boy.
It's like the echo of the Devil's long last laugh.
It tastes like cold soup that was made two years ago.
It smells like dog droppings that haven't been picked up.
It feels like a hard old wrinkly person's skin.
It looks like you haven't got any sense of humour and you're about
to explode
Now you've learnt how girls react when they are angry.

James Masson (9)
Fraserburgh South Park School, Fraserburgh

Anger

It's red like the darkest swirling blood from a human.
It sounds like the loud roar from a lion.
It tastes like red-hot spicy chilli sauce.
It smells like burning black toast.
It feels like the hottest water in the world.
It looks like a rampaging bull; I think I'm going to *explode!*

Aaren Cooper (10)
Fraserburgh South Park School, Fraserburgh

Anger

It is red like hot burning lava bursting from a volcano.
It sounds like roaring thunder that's dying to lash with rain.
It tastes like a red-hot pepper burning in my mouth.
It smells like jet-black smoke blocking up my nostrils.
It feels like a very hard and rough mountain.
It looks like a wild bull out of control.
It's growing as you read this.

Fiona Bruce (9)
Fraserburgh South Park School, Fraserburgh

The Alligator

A mouth like a snapping mousetrap
Teeth like a sharp chainsaw blade
Its claws are like a crab moving stealthily
Skin like slimy snakes
Eyes like jet black beady marbles
Tail like a pointed sharp knife
It glides through the water like a flaming bullet
I think I'm about to faint.

Jade Kay (9)
Fraserburgh South Park School, Fraserburgh

The Alligator

A mouth like a cold creepy dark cane
Teeth like a mean lean fighting machine
Claws like a samurai sword
Skin like a silly old rattlesnake
Eyes are jet-black beady crystals
Tail like a whipping highwayman
It's like a bulldozer going through water
I've just found my favourite creature.

Luke Maitland (9)
Fraserburgh South Park School, Fraserburgh

The Alligator

Teeth like a razor-sharp butcher's knife
Mouth like a cold creepy dark cave
Claws like a fishing hook
Skin like a rough volcano
Eyes jet-black beady dark marbles
Tail, it whips like a highwayman
It hunts down its prey like a professional hunter
I felt like I would faint.

Ian Neilson (9)
Fraserburgh South Park School, Fraserburgh

The Alligator

A mouth like a cold creepy cave
Lots of sharp, slimy, slithery teeth
Claws like sharp pointy fishing rods
Lumpy skin that looks like stone slimy tiles
Eyes that are dark beady marbles
A horrible, lashing, waving tail that lashes towards its prey
It slumbers and rips its prey open to eat his food
I feel I would jump out of my skin.

Katie Armstrong (9)
Fraserburgh South Park School, Fraserburgh

The Alligator

The mouth is like scissors snapping shut.
The teeth are like sharp pencils.
The claws are painted to dig into its prey.
The eyes are jet-black beads.
The skin is like burnt toast.
The tail, it is like a big wart.
It is lazy, walking on land.
I am very scared of the alligator.

Stephen Park (9)
Fraserburgh South Park School, Fraserburgh

Anger

It is red like blood running through a boy
It is a roaring sound like a starving lion
It tastes like sea water out at the beach
It smells like revolting rotten eggs
It feels like turf on a football park
It looks like a mad cow chasing a person
Look out, it's crazy!

Jackie Adams (9)
Fraserburgh South Park School, Fraserburgh

Anger

It is red like the fear of a werewolf.
It sounds like a blazing blade of a knight.
It tastes like red-hot chilli sauce.
It smells like a stinky stink bomb.
It feels like scrappy sandpaper.
It looks like a sabre tooth tiger ripping its prey.

Andrew John Summers (10)
Fraserburgh South Park School, Fraserburgh

Emperor Penguin - Haiku

Emperor penguin
Swimming in the icy sea
Looking for fat fish.

Daniel Ross (10)
Fraserburgh South Park School, Fraserburgh

The Squid - Haiku

The soft squishy squid
It is big, long and dotty
Lives in cold water.

Marc Summers (10)
Fraserburgh South Park School, Fraserburgh

The Penguin - Haiku

Majestic penguin
Shoots through the sea like a hawk
Catches his big fish.

Mark Tait (9)
Fraserburgh South Park School, Fraserburgh

Under The Sea

The clear, blue, sparkling sea is
A thick ancient book with unstoppable crimpled pages
Filled with mysteries and excitement.
The clear, blue, sparkling sea is
Swaying as gently and as calmly as clouds
In the bright, beautiful, blue sky.
The clear, blue, sparkling sea is
As deep as a ravine in the Pacific Ocean
Overlooking the sands of California.

The clear, sparkling, blue sea is
Happily smiling with joyful excitable glee
As the magnificent speedboat race begins.
The clear, sparkling, blue sea is
Like furious rapids rushing speedily along
Like a boiling hot volcano about to explode.
The clear sparkling sea is
As blue as light paint
Being tenderly and patiently stroked over the smooth walls.

Ythan Johnson (10)
Glenlivet Primary School, Ballindalloch

Floyd Mayweather - The Boxer

The blood poured down his face like a little stream pouring gently
from his split eyelid.
His sweat dripped off his battered nose like he had been in a fierce
and dangerous river.
His rock-hard mouthpiece flew out of his mouth with great force
Like it had been blown out with vicious explosives.
His swollen cheek was like a massive, unforgiving stone boulder.
His opponent's glove was split with the monstrous and powerful
punches that he thrust at him.
His chin was covered with thick red blood.
His right arm was purple from the pain and exhaustion of delivering
his merciless blows.

Daniel Balfour (10)
Glenlivet Primary School, Ballindalloch

My Home

Outside my window
The silver moon yawns as it puts everyone to sleep.
Outside my window
The trees undress their warmth of leaves as they dance
and flutter to the ground.
Outside my window
The breeze was as lovely as a newly baked cake just taken
out of the smouldering oven
With its warmth surrounding me.
I look outside my window, it's full of life.
Outside my window
The wind sings a lovely little song to me.
Outside my window
The bloom seems to follow on through the woods as the flowers
sing to themselves.
Outside my window
It's quiet, as quiet as the silent star that calls your name.
I look outside my window; I wouldn't swap it for the world.

Outside my window
The beauty calls to me like an angel that has the most
spectacular wings.
Outside my window
The wind has a warming touch that fills my heart with joy.
Outside my window
The animals jump and leap as tall as the tops of the trees.
I look outside my window; it's so special to me.

Emily West (10)
Glenlivet Primary School, Ballindalloch

Hate

Hate is an outrageous volcano with boiling lava in the burning sun
Hate is a red-hot chilli burning tongues of joy and happiness.
Hate is God when He is angrily striking the world like a bomb.
Hate, why was it made?

Hate is a bullet killing people from the furious sky above.
Hate is a hurricane bashing everything down disastrously
and nothing left.
Hate is like thunder striking its victims from above which is a blood
of death.

Hate where was it made?

Hate is a death book thundering to the ground and has blood
running out of it.
Hate is a crooked house slowly dying to the ground with a burning fire.
Hate is like the moon thrashing to the Earth.
Hate, how was it made?

Millie Clethero (8)
Glenlivet Primary School, Ballindalloch

The Springtime

In the morning of spring, the sky shines as light as a spyglass
looking at the sun.
In the morning of spring a bird is as gorgeous as the
Mediterranean Sea.
In the morning of spring the river sparkles happily like a ruby.
I love the spring, it is so great, I never get bored, I open
up my fantasy world.

In the afternoon of spring the sun goes down like a flower with no water.
In the afternoon of spring more life is born every day on the farm.
In the afternoon of spring the rabbits nibble on the rich and succulent
lettuce that the farmer grows.
I love spring, it is so great, I never get bored, I open up
my fantasy world.

Forest Lawson (11)
Glenlivet Primary School, Ballindalloch

Outside My Window

Outside my window it looks so beautiful.
Outside my window I would never change it.
Outside my window I can see purple heather all over the hills.
Outside my window I can see all the new animals wake up and yawn.
Outside my window I can see my brother going to school.
Outside my window I can see the river running.
Outside my window I can see if it is raining hard.
Outside my window I can see my dad go to work.
Outside my window I can see frogs laying frogspawn.
Outside my window I can see the hall lights going up for Hallowe'en.
Outside my window I can see big fat pheasants.
Outside my window I can see beautiful snowdrops.
Outside my window I can see fantastic fireworks.
Outside my window it looks so beautiful.
Outside my window I would never change it.

Campbell Adamson (8)
Glenlivet Primary School, Ballindalloch

The Black Stallion

The black stallion is as sharp as a cool metal tack.
The black stallion's mane is a cascading flowing river of death.
The black stallion is a shock of thunder as she runs.
The black stallion has a paradise home in a big luxury cave.
The black stallion is beautiful; I wouldn't change her I wouldn't try.

The black stallion is as fast as lightning stealing through the desert.
The black stallion is a furious fighter as she fights for her life against
the cheetah.
The black stallion is the queen of all horses as she stands proud
and tall,
When she neighs her echo is heard all over the world.
The black stallion is amazing all the time; I wouldn't change her, I
wouldn't try.

Katie Durno (8)
Glenlivet Primary School, Ballindalloch

Spring Has Come

Outside my window the crystal-white snowdrops were moving quickly
like they were forming an army.
Outside my window the children were lions as they ran around
ferociously to find Easter eggs.
Outside my window the little fluffy lambs fell over
like a soft sleepy pillow.
Outside my window, I would not change it for the world.

Outside my window the blossom are falling gracefully
like a parachute from the green trees.
Outside my window the rabbits are drinking like a vacuum,
sucking up all the sweet water from the glistening puddles.
Outside my window the beautiful flowers are as lovely
as a sparkling river flowing softly away from the stream.
Outside my window, I would not try and change it, ever!

Outside my window the daisies are shooting out of the ground
like bullets.
Outside my window the salmon are racing like a small rocket car
to claim the prize of the river.
Outside my window the daffodils are as creamy as a yellow tin of paint.
Outside my window, I could not change it for the world!

Lucinda Lock (9)
Glenlivet Primary School, Ballindalloch

The Beautiful Summer

Outside my window the sparkly river laughed into the summer warmth
As it blew the air to warm it up.
Outside my window the elastic sky woke with a stretch
                                    into the early morning.
Outside my window the big monstrous mountains yawned
                                    and said goodnight.
Outside my window, it's beautiful like the morning sun.

Outside my window the flowers drink the water of the night
                                    as it they were alive.
Outside my window the wind is whistling a merry tune through the day.
Outside my window the smooth stones glitter like they are bottles
                                    in the sun.
Outside my window, it's beautiful like the wild flowers.

Outside my window the fish are bullets as they fly through the rapid
                                    water flow.
Outside my window the twittering birds are a choir as they sign
                                    magnificently on the tree.
Outside my window the trees are as wild as a powerful cat
                                    in the jungle.
Outside my window, it's beautiful like all the different birds in the trees.

Miles Thomas (10)
Glenlivet Primary School, Ballindalloch

Who Am I?

A cake baker
A sports lover
A house settler
A life saver
A loving respecter
A child saver
A funny adventurer
A cool character
A secret keeper
A night sleeper
A daytime dreamer
A tea drinker
A life freezer
A hard worker

Did you guess?
I am Granny from Hoodwinked.

Lauren McHardy (9)
Glenlivet Primary School, Ballindalloch

Splish Splash

What am I?

A fire starter
A plant grower
A damp boarder
A cat destroyer
A tree helper
A river flower
A chilly icer
A fun splasher
A chlorine filler
A cloud maker

I am water!

Emma Durno (10)
Glenlivet Primary School, Ballindalloch

My Cool Year

Spring is so cool . . .
New animals are born every minute
Easter eggs are scattered everywhere
So you can find sweet delicious chocolate eggs
In spring beautiful sunsets come down to become night.

Summer is so cool . . .
It is like a burning meteor crashing down to Earth
Bees are creating sweet honey to eat
Rivers are crashing down like waterfalls
And the fantastic blue sky is like the colour of the sea.

Autumn is so cool . . .
It is as cold as a tap that has just been turned on
Leaves fall from the thick brown trees
And the wind is stronger than a sumo wrestler.
Hallowe'en is very scary but full of delicious sweets.

Winter is so cool . . .
Winter is colder than the North Sea
The snow is deep, deeper than the foundations of a shed,
And the birds are going south to keep warm.

Luke Middleton (8)
Glenlivet Primary School, Ballindalloch

The Fire

The fire is like a pouncing tiger
Beautiful but deadly, sharp and unsteady
Lazing around all day until *wham!*
Its eyes glow like orange embers
The horror of watching it strike.
You can see a glimpse of the blood red killing machine
And then you see nothing but the horror in its eyes.
The beast is dying down into ashes,
The horror, horror, horror is asleep again.

Callum Robert Stewart (11)
Grantown Primary School, Grantown-on-Spey

The Volcano

The volcano is a raging dragon
Big and dangerous.
He sleeps for a long time
And awakens in a rage.

Anger is flowing,
Now he is dangerous.
He starts to roar,
Time is running out!

Lava is flowing down its side,
Roaring all the time.
Now it's hunting
For its dinner.

Destruction lies everywhere
Nothing moves.
He has had his dinner
And now he goes back to sleep.

Roy Gibson (11)
Grantown Primary School, Grantown-on-Spey

To A Mars Bar

Oh what a chunk of deliciousness
Look at that melting caramel
That smooth chocolate around the edges
And oh the fluffy sponge at the bottom.

I put you in the fridge
And then enjoy your cold chewiness
Or devour you on a hot summer day
Warm, gooey, runny caramel.

I only met you last year
So you come again and meet my teeth
And you will make my mouth water
I feel I'm in paradise.

Jessica Hart (11)
Grantown Primary School, Grantown-on-Spey

The Volcano

The volcano is a fiery tiger.
Fierce and orange
He stands at the top all day.
He has sparkling teeth and sharp claws.
Minute by minute he roars.

The red-hot rocks rolling away
And then the tiger explodes.
The tiger runs up and down the volcano
Licking himself clean
And then the moon pops out of nowhere.

Then the storm blows out
He jumps to his feet and looks for prey
But then he hides away out of the storm.
The bubbly lava starts to rise again,
The tiger stops and then runs.

Ashes start to fall from the sky
Boom! The tiger explodes again,
The tiger runs and runs and just escapes.

Callum Cockman (11)
Grantown Primary School, Grantown-on-Spey

To A Tube Of Smarties

Oh you round beautiful Smartie
You are red, green, brown, purple and orange
You are as small as a button.

I eat you one by one while I watch BBC One
I leave the orange ones till last
You are my Friday treat
I look forward to you all week.

You are squashed in a colourful tube
Ready for me to pop you open
You melt in my mouth and I crunch the shell
Hurry up Friday.

Andrew Cooke (11)
Grantown Primary School, Grantown-on-Spey

To An Apple Crumble

Oh what a beautiful apple crumble
How perfect you look
Your smell is warming up the house
The sugar looks like snow sprinkled on the top.

The excitement is unbearable
You make my mouth water
I dig into the gorgeous apple crumble
And slowly put it into my mouth.

Then it melts away slowly
I bite into the crumble
It's sweet and crunchy
You are delicious.

You remind me of birthdays
You've been my favourite dish since I was little.
It's all gone now
The best food ever!

Kate Masson (11)
Grantown Primary School, Grantown-on-Spey

A Volcano

A volcano is an angry dragon
Huge and grey,
It sleeps for a long time
Steam coming out of its nose.

After the beast awakens
Flames shoot out of its mouth
Violent in every way
Destroying all that is in its way
And roars all day long.

The monster destroys
All of the life that is near
Making sacred blazes of fire
Wrecking people's homes.

Scott Rose (11)
Grantown Primary School, Grantown-on-Spey

To A Crunchy

Oh what a lovely Crunchy
Your nice crispy centre
And wonderful chocolate outside
When I open the gold wrapper.

You make me smile
When I bite your
Centre, it is so yummy
The chocolate it melts in my mouth.

When I look at you
I am delighted that I can have you
I bite you and my tummy feels so good
Like a butterfly is in it.

I can't wait till I can have you again
Hopefully I can eat you today
And will enjoy eating your crunchy taste
Your lovely chocolatey taste.

Alan Scott (11)
Grantown Primary School, Grantown-on-Spey

The Volcano

A volcano is an angry red dragon
Breathing heavily on the hill
Just waiting for something to waken it up.

And in a stormy day in October
He is waking and *roars!*
The giant red dragon has woken up.

Top of the volcano
It's rising up, up,
Suddenly up comes the fire and lava.

It calmly settles down
Back into his deep sleep
Until the next time he wakes.

Harry Craig (11)
Grantown Primary School, Grantown-on-Spey

The Earthquake

The earthquake is an angry elephant
Giant and grey
Stamping in the forest all day
With his huge feet and swaying trunk
He rules the woods.

His scary, fierce, beady eyes
Look around for something to destroy
As he pounds and bounds
Through the woods
All the trees are swaying.

People stop, look, listen, then run
Nobody knows what to say or where to go
They scatter in shock
Leaving their loved ones
Crying fills the air.

Suddenly there is silence
Everything has stopped
No movement at all
As he slowly calmly walks away
He goes to sleep for another day!

Yandra Banks Brown (11)
Grantown Primary School, Grantown-on-Spey

Newborn Puppies

So scared and small
Their golden coat shining in the sun
Soft, fluffy, mini and cute
Gobbling up their tasty dog biscuits
Play fighting with their brothers and sisters
Noisy kids shrieking in their floppy ears
So many new exciting smells
Running round the big new garden
Touching the new soft blanket
Sleeping with their mum at the end of the day.

Brighde Atkinson (9)
Grantown Primary School, Grantown-on-Spey

To A Yorkshire Pudding

Oh you beautiful Yorkshire pudding
How wonderful you look today
Smartly dressed
In thick dripping brown gravy.

You smell moist and delicious
I just can't wait to gobble you, and then wait
To feel your light centre slide down my throat
And crunch on your crispy coating.

When I think of you, I feel warm inside
You make my tummy rumble
I can feel you steaming on the plate
Oh, you make me smile.

You've always been my favourite
My friend, my one and only
If my granny didn't cook you on a Sunday
What would I do? A disaster!

I eat you slowly to savour you
I'm nearly finished my plate
Oh how good you taste
Please come back soon, don't be late.

Holly Dunbar (11)
Grantown Primary School, Grantown-on-Spey

Cats

Playful jumping cats
Zooming happy cats
Sleeping cats
From running around all day
Sitting at the door
Wishing all day that I would come back
Cats climbing trees
All colours
Very soft cats.

Charlotte McKee (9)
Grantown Primary School, Grantown-on-Spey

Ode To A Hot Chocolate

Oh you beautiful hot chocolate
You look really tasty
Look at those marshmallows
Melting on to the cream
I am so relaxed thinking about you.

Slowly drinking hot chocolate
A glow of warmth going down into my tummy
How comforting and warm you are
My face covered in cream.

Oh you hot chocolate, makes my tummy rumble
With those marshmallows dribbling off the sides
All that cream melting into the hot chocolate
You make me want to smile.

I remember when I was seven
When I first met you
You tasted delicious
It was such a treat.

Amber Hunter (11)
Grantown Primary School, Grantown-on-Spey

To A Plate Of Macaroni Cheese

Oh what a breathtaking experience
Oh we owe it to you
You make my mouth water when I think
About your soft pasta with dripping crispy cheese.

You are my old friend
You make me smile with your cheesy pasta
I've loved you since I was a little girl
Every time I taste your beautiful flavour
It makes my tummy rumble
It's lovely how I can drool over you
My lovely macaroni.

Kristin Currie-Jones (11)
Grantown Primary School, Grantown-on-Spey

To A Lasagne

Oh what a beautiful lasagne on thy plate,
You look so tasty covered in cheese.
You make me drool thinking about you,
It makes my tummy rumble talking about you.

Now I will eat you,
I adore how you taste when I take a bite.
It makes my mouth water when I swallow you,
Oh how lovely in my stomach.

I want you every night and day,
Oh how I will miss you.
How I love your smell
And I miss it.

Farewell lasagne,
I will always miss you
You lovely lasagne,
Oh how tasty.

Ben Fitzhugh (11)
Grantown Primary School, Grantown-on-Spey

To A Malteser!

Oh you beautiful Malteser how tasty you look today.
You little ball of joy,
You're smooth outside and your wonderful crispy centre,
Yes, you are the best thing ever.

I will eat you as slowly as possible so I can enjoy your inner self.
You smell as if you are a freshly picked flower.
I'm totally in love with you, your beauty,
My mouth is always watering when I see you.

I remember when I met you; it was love at first sight.
You are my dream and my life,
When I see you I hope you will be my wife.

Now it's time to say goodbye, I will buy you again later
But now I will eat you, I'll see you later.

Tom Strang (11)
Grantown Primary School, Grantown-on-Spey

To A Hot Chocolate

Oh you beautiful hot chocolate
Look at your creamy topping
With marshmallows dripping from you
And with lots of colourful small sprinkles.

You make my tummy rumble
Every time I see you
And you carry me away with the
Beautiful smell.

I see you disappearing
So now I think it's time,
Time to drink you
I will miss you, bye-bye hot chocolate.

When will I see you again?
You have not always been my friend
But now you are.
You make me feel as if I own the world.

You remind me of Christmas
And snow so I hope I have you
Tomorrow and just the same
Goodbye, goodbye.

Lauren Simpson (11)
Grantown Primary School, Grantown-on-Spey

Nature All Around Us

Green grass growing all around us
Wind whistling through the tall trees
Blue sparkling water swishing and slow flowers
Beautiful pink and purple perfumed flowers
Raindrops making leaves on the trees sparkle and plopping
                                                in the puddles

Birds chirping loudly from the branches
Nature makes me feel so happy and excited.

Alex Whiller (8)
Grantown Primary School, Grantown-on-Spey

To A Chocolate Spread

Beautiful chocolate spread
You are chocolatey and runny
The best on a croissant from France
Spread thick and tasty.

You make my mouth water
I have to eat you before my tummy rumbles
I enjoy you so much you make me smile
Milky chocolate melts in my mouth.

I have to eat you straight away
How glad I am to meet you
I wish I knew you before I tasted you
You're as beautiful as the queen.

You're in my pack lunch today,
I can't wait to eat you.
You are so yummy in my tummy,
I'll miss you.

Jason Gordon (11)
Grantown Primary School, Grantown-on-Spey

Kenny The Snake

My snake Kenny
He's silver, brown and grey,
Eating smelly mice
Swallowing them whole.
Slithering on the floor,
Resting under the couch,
Playing with Razor
My brother's snake.
Hiding in my shirt,
Big and fat because of his mice,
Swimming in the tub.

Jordan O'Donnell (9)
Grantown Primary School, Grantown-on-Spey

Ode To A Hot Dog

Oh what beautiful food you are.
How smart you are,
How smartly dressed up today
And your beautiful sausage in the middle with onions and ketchup.

I feel very happy when I eat you.
Oh you nice hot dog, I feel happy when I watch you,
You are waiting for me to eat you.

When I'm hungry
I think of you and my mouth goes all watery.
I love your savoury hot taste
Ketchup squelches in my mouth.

Mate Szinyeri (11)
Grantown Primary School, Grantown-on-Spey

The Volcano

The volcano is an angry dragon
Tall and scaly
He groans on the hill all day
With his steaming nose and pointed teeth
Hour upon hour he snores.

With his rumbling thundering tummy
He wakes up and roars
Fire shooting out of his jaw
As he gnaws
On the helpless Earth.

Then he relaxes
And goes back to sleep
Now everything's quiet
Until next time he wakes.

Eilidh Sutherland (11)
Grantown Primary School, Grantown-on-Spey

The Volcano

The volcano is a hungry tiger
Huge and orange
With his sparkling teeth
And sharp claws.
Hour upon hour he roars.

The bubbling lava down below
With the rocks ready to blow.
Tiger spots his meal tonight
And then pounces on his prey
Yum, yum and walks away.

The roaring of the tiger and
Boom goes the lava.
The destruction is done
So quiet, so sad,
The tiger moves on with destruction on his face.

Sonas Walker (11)
Grantown Primary School, Grantown-on-Spey

WWE Raw

Wide ring
Ready for fighting
Shouting people
Wrestling's exciting
Big twirling round
Wrestlers rolling on the ground
Spine buster bending backs
Swanton bomb
Diving down attacks
Knuckle shuffle
You can't see me
Bouncing off the ropes
With his knee
Ping . . . one . . . two . . . three . . .
Ding! Ding! Ding!
The wrestler's victory!

Shaun Grant (10)
Grantown Primary School, Grantown-on-Spey

My Messy Bedroom!

My bedroom is really warm.
I can still smell my perfume
I sprayed a few weeks ago!
It is amazingly messy but I have cool posters that are hanging
from the wall.

I have cool curtains hanging from the wall,
Loud CD players coming out of the room,
Shoes flying out of my wardrobe,
Clothes pinging out of my room.
I have got a nice colour of walls,
It looks cool!

Leanne Grant (9)
Grantown Primary School, Grantown-on-Spey

To A Marshmallow

Oh what a creamy thing so hot over the fire and as brown
as chocolate.
It makes my mouth water and I gasp smelling you.
You were my friend when I was little and you still are.
Next when I see you it's on the hot barbeque at my house
on my birthday.

Heidi Dickson (11)
Grantown Primary School, Grantown-on-Spey

Football

Big rectangular pitch with smooth green grass
A black and white football that goalkeepers dive for
Cheering crowds, players whacking the ball
Referee's whistle is blowing, their team wins the FA Cup.

Cari Palomino (8)
Grantown Primary School, Grantown-on-Spey

My Bedroom

My bedroom is very, very messy
In my bedroom there are clothes everywhere,
Piles and piles of shoes for me to trip over.
The walls are a pretty pink colour and it smells of
Rock 'n' Rose perfume.
There are cool posters on the wall.
I have the most comfy bed in the world.
The pink walls feel smooth; my bedroom makes me feel cool.

Ashley Emma Rose (10)
Grantown Primary School, Grantown-on-Spey

Snowy The Snake

My snake Snowy is white with orange spots
He climbs up the vines,
He swims in the bath,
He slithers and hides up my sleeves,
He coils tightly round my tree, sneaking under the bark.
He strikes his prey
And swallows a mouse in one big *gulp!*

Darren Gilfillan (10)
Grantown Primary School, Grantown-on-Spey

Athletics

I really like athletics
Olympic champions ready to start
Smelly sweat dripping from their forehead
People zooming past
Costumes white and grey
Runners winning medals
Winners they have one.

Annabelle Fraser (9)
Grantown Primary School, Grantown-on-Spey

Rock 'N' Roll

Noisy drums making a racket
Brand new electric guitars
Take them out of the packet
Singing girls and boys
Rock 'n' roll isn't a toy
Tall microphones and people's voices
Making lots of noise
Back-up bass guitar
If you play it right you will go far
Fast dancing with magic moves
Not to mention groovy groves
It's pure rock 'n' roll.

Caitie Fitzhugh (9)
Grantown Primary School, Grantown-on-Spey

Football Crazy

Giant stadium
Footballers sweating
Noisy rattles
Fans are shouting very loud
Different coloured football strips on the football pitch
The game is over, Manchester United scored.

Ross Wilson (8)
Grantown Primary School, Grantown-on-Spey

My Flower

This flower means a lot
It is the only flower in a pot.
I keep it fresh every day
It sits still on my windowsill.
It helps me get to sleep at night
It's so cool, I see it bright.

Hannah Sinclair (10)
Grantown Primary School, Grantown-on-Spey

Noisy Classroom

People shouting
Pencils scribbling
Sellotape ripping
Chairs screeching
Computers clicking
Scissors cutting
Teachers nagging
Sssh!

Joe Dunbar **(9)**
Grantown Primary School, Grantown-on-Spey

Basketball

Whistle blows
Bouncing a ball
Shoot for the hoop
The cheering crowd
Aim at the square
Running up and down
Sharp passing
Sweaty forehead.

Clay Chisholm **(9)**
Grantown Primary School, Grantown-on-Spey

My Basketball

My basketball is round
It is a very special ball
It bounces very high
It grips to your hand like sticky gum
People dribbling on the tar
People throwing and catching
Scoring through the hoops
The win, the cup.

Andrew John Stewart **(9)**
Grantown Primary School, Grantown-on-Spey

PlayStation Zombie

My wide eyes are stuck to the screen
Never going to school
Because the PlayStation rules!

Loads of buttons to press
But I won't give it a rest.

Saving data
The memory card's full
The game that I am playing
Is ever so cool.

Sam Cockman (9)
Grantown Primary School, Grantown-on-Spey

Cheeseburger

Cheeseburgers are hot
Fresh from the grill
With a crispy bun
And greasy meat, *yum!*
They're a gift from Heaven
It's really true,
They're top of the menu.
The chefs are frying,
Customers are buying,
Cheeseburgers are tasty.

Jack Tulloch (9)
Grantown Primary School, Grantown-on-Spey

Heavenly Hot Chocolate

Heavenly hot chocolate
Always warm and moist
Tasty melting marshmallows
Bubbling to and fro
Rippling beautifully round the mug
Always warming up your throat
When you *glug!*
Bubbling brown chocolate
It feels so burny hot
Just poured from the pot.

Ben Allan (9)
Grantown Primary School, Grantown-on-Spey

Lola The Rabbit

L is for lots of fluff waiting to give me a hug
O is for one loveable rabbit that is my friend
L is for a lovely rabbit that is my soul
A is for a bond that we share, it is the best thing in my life

T is for the love between us, it will never disappear
H is for her and I will never be parted
E is for even when she dies, I will remember the times

R is for rare happiness to me and to her it will stay
A is for as she hops her heart gets bigger
B is for behold this great love we have
B is for best thing in the whole world
I is for love that we share every day
T is for too good of a bond that cannot be replaced.

Morgan Potter (12)
Hatton (Cruden) Primary School, Peterhead

The Playground

Argh!
Voices shout and echo
Like explorers escaping terrifying tigers
In the playground jungle!
Enormous elephants,
Stomp, stomp,
Stomping starving giant!
Silver paper
Rip, rip,
Like children scraping knees.
Here I come
Like cavemen hunting their quest,
Ouch!
People scream and shout
Tackling rugby players!
The playground is a fun place,
Is yours?

Olivia Paddock (10)
Hatton (Cruden) Primary School, Peterhead

Playground

The playground is like a breath of fresh air,
Space, black and shiny,
Whoa, whoa, yeah, yeah!
Falls, football, fun, faults.
The playground, the playground,
The playground, the playground,
Everyone loves the playground
Apart from arguments!
Play is all we think about
In rain, snow, sun or wind.
Everyone loves the playground,
Toddler, adult, teenager or child,
It's safe and fun,
How much more of a bargain can you get?

Luke Radford (10)
Hatton (Cruden) Primary School, Peterhead

The Playground

The slide is the playground
Children playing go, 'Argh! Ha ha. Argh! Ha ha'
Children happy, happy, helpful, la la
Boys firing guns *bang, boom, bang, boom!*
Girls dancing, singing, screaming
Playground helpers first aiding oh, ouch, oh, ouch!
Slidy whoosh, whee oh!
Shouting, crying, singing and screaming
Like a mix of emotions, gives everyone a fright
The football pitch is a rock solid ball
This causes trouble
The noise gets louder as cool cars pass
The loud bell rings *bring, bring!*
Everyone rushes to their lines wanting to be first
In the classroom is silence
Well, doesn't that make you think?

Kirsty Clark (10)
Hatton (Cruden) Primary School, Peterhead

Playground

The monster of the playground will eat you up!
Towering trees blow from side to side,
Leaves fall from the sky, crunch, crunch!
The children are monkeys jumping about,
The footballers are shouting,
The playground is quiet, when the bell goes.
There are children racing about everywhere.
The playground is dark at night,
The playground is like the moon at night,
The playground surface is as dark as space,
The trees are monsters chasing you about,
The playground is a trampoline.
Suddenly, silence then
Ring, ring, ring!
Everyone is running inside.

Callum Duncan (11)
Hatton (Cruden) Primary School, Peterhead

Playgrounds

Bounce, boing, bounce, boing,
Happy children are dashing everywhere
Like crazy dogs.
Whisper, giggle, ssh, whisper, giggle, ssh,
Two best friends are sharing secrets.
Primary ones prancing about
Not looking where they're going,
Running faster and faster until
Crash!
Munch, crunch, gobble, gulp,
Yummy snacks
Making your tummy rumble.
Goal! The older boys
Are watching a tense game of football
Like lions with bulging eyes
Watching an easy catch.
Bring, bring, bring!
The bell is ringing
For the end of playtime,
Everyone rushing to be first.
Everyone files in,
A few minutes later
Silence.
This is what goes on in my playground,
What about yours?

Sarah Dignan (10)
Hatton (Cruden) Primary School, Peterhead

Playground

A playground is a huge funfair
So many things to do
Bouncing
High up on the see-saw splash! Splash!
Wet weather
Children huddle together
Watch out for the ball
Bash!
You're hit
Whoosh!
Whizzing by on the swings
Running, jumping, bouncing
Energetic kids
Constantly tripping up
What clumsy clowns
Screaming, shouting
Kids are rather loud
They are headless chickens
Running around mad
Bla, bla, bla
Non-stop talking
Until . . .
Bring!
Kids scurry to their lines
The playground is dead.

Beth Stevenson (11)
Hatton (Cruden) Primary School, Peterhead

The Playground

The playground is full of kids running around
Whea, yeah, tig!
The climbing frame is like a shiny mirror,
Newly polished, gleaming in the sun.
The slide is a zipwire
But it is like a mini ski slope.
The bin is like a merry monster
Ready to gobble up
Litter and anyone causing it.
The flowerpots are beautiful, miniature
Gardens, hand grown by professionals.
The football goals are like a silvery spider's web
Ready to swallow the ball.
The weather is always sunny
Like on a slippery, slidey, scorching seaside.
The toys bring as much joy to a child
As all their favourite toys piled high on Christmas.
The play equipment brings lots of joy,
A pirate's ship, all aboard, ahoy!
A pond glistening in the sun,
As blue as a blanket you sleep on
A beautiful bench just like a settee is just the perfect place for me.
The trees are as tall as giraffes
And add beauty to the scenery.
The playground helpers are as strict as Victorian teachers.
The gate was painted just by me
Not yellow but pink and not pale green.
The pebbles are beautiful, shiny and white,
They shine like pearls in the light.
Let's take a ride on the zipwire,
Zip, whoa, yeah!
The roundabout goes around like a whirlwind
This playground is full of glee
Perhaps it's the perfect playground for me.

Lauren Kyle (11)
Hatton (Cruden) Primary School, Peterhead

Our Playground

Children running, playing,
Like a lion chasing a zebra, grrr!
People sitting being bored
Like a herd of sheep wondering
What part of the grass is the nicest, hmm.
Children charging all day long
Like a pack of wild animals fighting, grrr.
Children playing hide-n-seek
Like a group of hunters chasing a fox, get it, kill it!
Children daring each other
'I dare you to climb the wall.' 'No, no, no!'
A group of children going on
A big bike ride
Like a stunt bike going vroom, vroom!
The playground is a big bubble of playing children.
Yabadabadoo!

Calum Murray (10)
Hatton (Cruden) Primary School, Peterhead

A Poem About Me

I am a chain on a motorbike zooming, zooming and zooming round
a track like a leopard.
I am sunglasses getting used twenty-four-seven
Then, when it is time for bed, I jump in and am nice and cosy
like a penguin.
I am a spanner getting cranked, cranked and cranked up into the air
like a rocket.
I am a motorbike flying and flying around a track at one-hundred miles
an hour like a lion.
I am a bit of a horse biting my food crunching in the morning
like a lion biting its prey.

Dean Mcleod (12)
Hatton (Cruden) Primary School, Peterhead

Playground

A playground is like a huge funfair,
Giggle, giggle, yeah!
Where you may meet your friends.
The playground is a huge blackboard
With letters darting around in circles,
Hurrah, hurrah, hurrah!
A playground is a big trampoline
Bong, bong, bong.
Bouncing right up to the sky
The playground is a busy city
With cars zooming past,
Vroom, vroom, vroom
Going as fast as they can.
A playground is a big black brick,
It's hard and painful if you fall
Boo hoo, boo hoo, boo hoo!

Sean Buchan (11)
Hatton (Cruden) Primary School, Peterhead

Playground

Deserted crows fly off
Bell rings, children come outside
They play happily
Teams for games are picked
Swings, climbing frame and football
Fresh air, fun and laughter
Shouting, screaming, some crying
Children aware of sounds, the bell could ring
Teacher, play nicely
Gone, rain starts
Children run or ignore it
Bell rings noisily
Children run to lines
Tiptoe inside
Going in for teaching
Happily out of the rain.

Craig Paterson (11)
Hatton (Cruden) Primary School, Peterhead

Our Playground

Tolling bell
Children rustling
Outside
Huddling girls
Secluded corners
Whispers and giggles
'Johnny Depp', 'Orlando Bloom' bounce off walls
Typical girl stuff
Infants playing *bang!*
Girls play, cuddly dogs
Older boys think they rule
Rain pours again
Crows gather
School closes
Teens appear, locals complain, they scatter,
School silent until morning.

Grant Jamieson (12)
Hatton (Cruden) Primary School, Peterhead

Playground

A sunny day
On a deserted island
My new dream playground found.
Swings, slides, sports, spinning chairs and swimming pools.
Free zone,
It was like Cadonas but 900,000,000,000 times better.
My playground would have no rules, fights
And all you would see and hear would be laugher
Ha, ha, ha, hee, hee, hee!
It's brill,
It has luscious green grass and a pond to play in.
Play, laugh and learn,
Do what you want.
Consoles, sports or Barbie dolls.
Warm, wet, windy or wintry,
Surprising the playground is
You'll be surprised what's around the corner
But one thing is for sure,
You'll always find a friend for you.

Grant Anderson (10)
Hatton (Cruden) Primary School, Peterhead

The Playground

The world is a playground
The sea, the sky, the land.
Splash, animals jumping in and out of water,
Flap, flap, birds fly wildly in the light.
Footsteps running through long grass, the sun beating down.
Ponds filled with frogs,
Jungles filled with monkeys swinging here and there
Like children on monkey bars.
Rhinos charge like bullies.
Bong! Children bounce up and down like bunnies.
Children are like pandas munching away at food.
It turns to night; the sky is a blue blanket,
The sky is for bats and owls to play now.
The sea is gloomy black, the surface is bare,
The streets are ruled by gangs, their playground games are stones
and spray cans.
The children lie in their beds and dream of swings and slides,
The world is a playground.

Megan Cantlay (11)
Hatton (Cruden) Primary School, Peterhead

Playground

The playground is a racetrack with people running around everywhere.
The playground is a hiding place for when you are
playing hide-and-seek.
The playground is a noisy place with children chatting to each other.
The playground is a safe place with everyone seeing if you are OK.
The playground is a place where you meet up with all your friends.
The playground is a football place with goals being scored.
The playground is a trampoline with everyone jumping everywhere.
The playground is an aviary with children flying high.
The playground is an exciting jungle with everyone
exploring everywhere.
The playground is a black monster ready to gobble you up,
gobble, gobble.
The playground is a deserted desert when everyone is inside
doing work.
The playground is an ice rink with everyone skating around.
The playground is an artist's design with big blobs everywhere.
The playground is a play park with everyone playing nicely.
The playground is a big black puddle when it is raining.

Daniel Cantlay (11)
Hatton (Cruden) Primary School, Peterhead

Our Playground

Bouncing like baby bunnies
Screaming and shouting
The entire universe cheering on a singer
Our noise is unbearable
We are monsters, wild, crazy, *boo!* Suddenly we'll pop out
Crash! Someone has fallen
Dancing, singing when it's hot
Freezing cold, huddled together
Running freely, wind in our faces
On the swings, laughing, chuckling
Ha, ha!
Sliding down the chute
Whoosh!
Banging our bottoms on the see-saw
We are playful puppies, tails swinging
Race for space hoppers, bouncing like kangaroos non-stop
When suddenly we turn quiet
Bring, bring, bring!
Rush to lines like obedient robots
March inside leaving our playground
Quiet, empty,
Dead.

Amanda Finnie (11)
Hatton (Cruden) Primary School, Peterhead

A Playground

A playground is a place of fun like monkeys jumping in the sun.
A playground is an angry child being as loud as they can
and going wild.
An adult's playground is a place of quiet sitting in peace without a riot.
A see-saw is a rocking ship swaying to and fro,
Flowers are a jumble of colours all laid out in a row.
A slide is a slippery snake slidey and windy.
A swing is a rocket flying into space then flying in another direction
to a different place.
A playground is like a dolphin in the sea dancing around
and jumping with glee.
A roundabout is a spinning coin, everyone wants to come and join.
A tunnel is a hidey hole for moles to hide from every soul.
Playgrounds are a jungle when elephants come, they rumble.
Kids in a playground are always changing their minds, like fish
in the ocean making lots of motion.
A playground is where you relax during school, after doing work
that's really cruel
The sky is a birds' playground where they fly and sway in the wind
and play.
Running and jumping and skipping and hopping around and around
and flopping and bopping
Bring, bring, bring, the school bell rings, children run to the lines
Like a cheetah that's spotted some meat and is seeing
who they can beat.

Rachel Lees (11)
Hatton (Cruden) Primary School, Peterhead

The Playground

The playground is huge,
The children are like a crowd at a concert.
Big, small, young and old, all play a game,
Running, football, houses, all playing.
Some people on their own or with others,
Some use Vilene as a game.
They can also upset each other by making fun of each other.
In every inch of the playground everyone's behaviour changes.
In the little ones, people giggle and talk to each other,
In the big ones, they're bouncing and shouting.
There are also big ugly bullies
Each making someone's life miserable in every action .
The bullies are everywhere like a bug.
In the football pitch there is happiness,
Shouting at each other to pass the ball.
Roaring like a lion so they get a goal
When the bell goes, everyone goes back to work just as if
they never got out.

Ellis Swainston (11)
Hatton (Cruden) Primary School, Peterhead

The Playground

Everywhere is a playground
The land, sea and sky,
Wishing wells drop, splash splitter!
Boys play footie, run about,
Girls just chat and giggle
Pretty pink and pretty purple sitting in a row.
Skip, stamp, stumble down the hopscotch
'Yippee!' we all shout, running and jumping about.
After lunch, people swing as high as the sky
At night everything is still
You can only hear an owl tu-whit, tu-whoo.
The sunrises bright, the sight of a child running to the swings
Benches sit there bored and still,
Stone gravel everywhere.
The moon sparkles bright upon the trees,
The swings sway in the wind,
Five minutes later, peace is in the air.

Gillian Porter (11)
Hatton (Cruden) Primary School, Peterhead

Bionicle

He is green like a peapod,
He is black like the sky
And he likes to fly around.
His friend is red like fire,
He is black like a rock,
And he loves hot rocks.

Rees Donaldson (8)
Hatton (Fintray) Primary School, Aberdeen

Duck Stuck In Muck

Once there was a duck stuck in muck
Looking for a•mummy duck
The duck was stuck in the muck
For a really long time

The duck got sad
But poor little duck got stuck in the muck
Then along came a buck and helped little duck
But poor duck was still stuck in the muck

The poor duck still stuck in the muck
Along came a bull and helped little duck
But poor little duck was still stuck in the muck

Oh poor duck can't get out of muck
Who will help him, who will?
Oh poor duck look here, look here
Along came a lion and a tiger

They helped little duck out of the muck
They pulled and pulled and pulled at duck
And little duck came out of the muck
And poor duck went home.

Phoebe Hone (9)
Hatton (Fintray) Primary School, Aberdeen

My Poem

The sunset is like a lovely crumpet
That the children like to eat with their feet.
The sun is yellow like a lovely meadow.

Rebecca Johnston Harman (7)
Hatton (Fintray) Primary School, Aberdeen

Emotions

Anger is red like a big flaming fire,
Happiness is white but the opposite of a fight,
Sadness is blue just a bit like you,
Scariness is black like a vampire bat.

Bruce Grant (8)
Hatton (Fintray) Primary School, Aberdeen

Amundsen And Scott

A dventurous explorer Amundsen,
M ade off to Antarctica.
U nwilling to be beaten,
N ever told anyone.
D id it secretly,
S et up camp.
E nded his mission,
N ow he is famous.

A mundsen was amazed to make it,
N otorious at the end.
D etermined to beat Scott.

S cott heard the race for the pole was on.
C ourageous men battling through blizzards.
O nly to find Amundsen had won.
T he Norwegian flag flying in the breeze.
T hey began their journey home devastated.

Angus MacLean (11)
Kennethmont Primary School, Huntly

Amundsen And Scott

A mazing explorer,
M r Roald Amundsen.
U nwilling to reveal his plans,
N ot mentioning his departure.
D eceived Scott, by
S ending him a message after he had left.
E nduring blizzards,
N ever giving up until he succeeded in reaching the pole.

And

S trong and brave,
C aptain Robert Scott.
O wed it to his companions,
T o battle through the blizzards,
T o reach the South Pole.

Morgan McCallum (11)
Kennethmont Primary School, Huntly

Amundsen And Scott

A Norwegian explorer
M any miles he travelled to the South Pole
U nder pressure to get there first
N ever giving up
D angerously cold temperatures
S nowstorms and blizzards
E very day
N ow he has achieved his goal

And

S cott was a British explorer
C ourageous and brave
O ff to the South Pole
T hough he didn't know
T hat Amundsen had beaten him.

Kyle Florence (11)
Kennethmont Primary School, Huntly

Amundsen And Scott

A n enthusiastic explorer
M ade his way to the South Pole
U naware of the circumstances
N ever spoke a word
D etermined to reach the South Pole
S et up camp in the cold
E xperienced in his work
N ever gave up on his journey

And

S cott was heading south
C arefully planning his route
O wed it to his companions
T o reach the South Pole
T hen they began their journey home.

Cara Simpson (11)
Kennethmont Primary School, Huntly

Amundsen And Scott

A ntarctica is where he was going
M agnificent person
U nafraid of dangers
N inety seven dogs
D etermined to reach the South Pole.
S kis he took
E xpert traveller
N orwegian explorer.

And

S hocked that Amundsen beat him
C ourageous all the way
O utstanding expedition
T he men and Scott died in the night
T hey will always be remembered.

Alex Jones (9)
Kennethmont Primary School, Huntly

Amundsen And Scott

A mundsen was determined to reach the South Pole first
M ade it there before Scott
U nder no circumstances would Amundsen give up
N ever will anyone be as brave
D etermination made Amundsen carry on through all the blizzards
S oon all the people in the world knew about his success
E xperience helped Amundsen get to the South Pole
N ow remembered for his achievement

And

S cott wanted to be the first to reach the South Pole
C ourage helped him succeed
O ver the years people have admired Scott's achievement
T hinking positive is the best thing to do all the time
T o work well together in harsh conditions is very good.

Jayne Duthie (9)
Kennethmont Primary School, Huntly

Amundsen And Scott

A ntartica adventurer
M arvellous person
U nexpected plans
N orwegian explorer
D angerous mission
S ecret trip to pole
E leven dogs survived after fifty seven days
N ever gave up

A ngry Scott
N ever knew
D evious Amundsen

S hocked Scott
C ourageous explorer made his plans
O ther men went with him
T rying hard to reach the pole
T hey died on the way back.

Beth MacLean (9)
Kennethmont Primary School, Huntly

Amundsen And Scott

A n amazing explorer,
M any miles he trekked,
U ndiscovered land he found,
N orwegian man,
D etermined to get to the South Pole,
S et sail in 1911,
E xplorer of the century,
N ever giving up,

And

S cott
C aptain Scott,
O h how he fought,
T o get to the pole,
T hrough bad conditions he travelled.

Esther Smith (9)
Kennethmont Primary School, Huntly

Amundsen And Scott

A mundsen was the first to reach the South Pole.
M ade it even though it was very, very cold.
U nhappy when he could not feel his hands or his feet.
N ever gave up so that was really, very brave.
D etermined to keep going no matter what.
S teady as he goes along and doesn't want to stop.
E xpert skiers to help move quickly.
N ever gave up so he managed to beat Scott

And

S cott wanted to be the first to reach the South Pole.
C ouldn't be more disappointed to see Amundsen's flag.
O utside in the cold he couldn't feel his hands.
T here he stood on top of the hill with a heavy heart.
T ried to be there first but Amundsen got there before him.

Rebecca Henderson (9)
Kennethmont Primary School, Huntly

Antarctica

A n explorer from Norway
M ust bring good equipment
U naware of bad weather
N eed to be brave
D angerous journey across the ice
S ure they'll survive
E ager to get to the pole
N eed to plant the Norwegian flag

And

S cott is a good explorer
C ourageous and brave
O ther explorers up ahead
T heir flag is there
T ime to go back.

Daniel Coursey (10)
Kennethmont Primary School, Huntly

Amundsen And Scott

A mundsen was an explorer.
M an who reached the South Pole and came back again.
U sed supplies and camped on the way.
N earer and nearer to the Pole every day.
D etermined to go on.
S afely and cautiously.
E xperienced in tackling arctic conditions.
N orway was his homeland.

And

S econd to the South Pole.
C onfident to win.
O ther men joined him.
T he men didn't make it back.
T hey died trying to conquer Antarctica.

Becky Jones (11)
Kennethmont Primary School, Huntly

To James McFadden

The Scottish campaign, ye played really well
Although in Italy ye were in yer shell
Against Faroe Islands ye were at yer best
You gave the defence a great big test
In Hampden when ye played France
You looked like you were doin' a dance
In Lithuania ye were OK
But ye didney play the Scottish way
In Paris ye made us very proud
When ye scored we a shouted out loud
A screaming curler against Ukraine
Showed your the man for the next campaign
The search is on for a leader oh the crowd
God help us all if it is Ally McLeod.

Harry Souttar (9)
Luthermuir Primary School, Laurencekirk

Love

Love sounds like birds tweeting.
Love smells like oozing chocolate.
Love feels like rabbit's fur.
Love tastes like seaside air.
Love looks like butterflies fluttering.
Love reminds me of my family.

Abbie Farquhar (8)
Luthermuir Primary School, Laurencekirk

Happiness

Happiness sounds like birds tweeting.
Happiness smells like freshly baked bread.
Happiness feels like a fluffy pillow.
Happiness looks like a newborn baby.
Happiness reminds me of my mam and dad.

Melissa Rodda (8)
Luthermuir Primary School, Laurencekirk

Happiness

Happiness sounds like the ice cream van slipping off
Happiness smells like strawberries dipped in chocolate sauce
Happiness feels like soft baby skin
Happiness tastes like a chocolate ripple
Happiness reminds me of fun days at the zoo.

Caera Grewar (9)
Luthermuir Primary School, Laurencekirk

Happiness

Happiness sounds like the KFC doors opening
Happiness smells like sausages sizzling in the pan
Happiness feels like tender chicken legs that are very hot
Happiness tastes like Victoria cake covered with jam
Happiness looks like the sun rising in the morning
Happiness reminds me of Disneyland Paris.

Sean Duncan (8)
Luthermuir Primary School, Laurencekirk

Happiness

Happiness sounds like the harp,
Happiness smells like freshly baked bread,
Happiness feels like Matilda, my guinea pig's fur
Happiness tastes as delicious as cheesecake
Happiness reminds me of my teacher, Mrs Watson.

Alexandra Grace Eavers (9)
Luthermuir Primary School, Laurencekirk

Fear

Fear sounds like the wailing of a banshee
Fear feels like icy breath
Fear smells like rotting flesh
Fear tastes like poison
Fear looks like darkness.

Calum McGuigan (9)
Luthermuir Primary School, Laurencekirk

The Dragon

There's a dragon in my bed
I think he ate my Ted.
I hear crunching
and munching
under my bed spread.

Samuel McGuigan (9)
Luthermuir Primary School, Laurencekirk

Aliens

A liens can be stripy or spotty everywhere,
L ook out! They are fearless so please be quite aware,
I have never seen one at night or during the day but,
E ven in the dark they can always find their way,
N oise is not a good idea, you might give them a fright,
S tep back! Don't hurt your eyes because they're very bright.

Hattie Sherlock (9)
Maud Primary School, Peterhead

Horses!

A pples, horses like to eat
B ranches they eat too
C arts horses pull them
D irty, clean and chubby horses are
E very horse is different
F at small, cute and cuddly
G rey, white, brown, black, dun, dapple lots of colours
H appy they are when they're getting fed
I absolutely adore them!
J ust having a trot
K itty cats don't always like horses
L ucky some horses are
M eadows to roam around in
N ewborn horses can be cheeky
O h but they're so beautiful
P retty horses I've got them
Q uads sometimes scare horses when they're riding
R iding is the best!
T raining horses can be fun
U is for the shape of their hooves
V ery good to groom
W hat a pretty animal
eX citing horses are!
Y ou better love them
Z oom, I will come chasing you if you don't.

Aimee Louise Mowat (9)
Maud Primary School, Peterhead

Seasons

S pringy lambs,
P retty flowers,
R unning children,
I n the sun.
N ot too cold.
G reen grass.

S wimming pools,
U mbrellas not needed.
M aximum heat,
M inimum cold.
E mergency ice cream required,
R ising sun looking beautiful.

A mazing coloured leaves.
U mbrellas definitely needed!
T all trees with no leaves.
U nder trees you will have to look out,
M aybe an acorn will fall on us!
N ot too warm I tell you!

W inning snowball fights.
I gloos getting made,
N o sunny days.
T hat's for sure!
E mergency hot chocolate required!
R ooftops covered with masses of snow.

Ainsley Morrison (10)
Maud Primary School, Peterhead

My Three Friends

I have three good friends,
They are really nice to me.
We like to go out places,
We'd even like to swim in the sea!

One of them is a bit annoying!
But I don't really mind,
Because she is still nice,
And really very kind!

One of them is funny,
She'd like to learn to climb.
She'd like me to teach her,
I would really like to, I just hope I have the time!

One of them is a bit silly,
She is always doing silly things.
I think she wants to fly,
Because she'd like some wings!

Those are my three friends,
Hattie, Heather and Moy!
Because they're such good friends I want to shout . . .
Oh boy! Oh boy! Oh boy!

Ellie Moore (9)
Maud Primary School, Peterhead

Me To You

M e to you teddies are the best!
E very one of them is cute and cuddly,

T hat's why my bedroom is full of me to yous!
O ver and over I'm smiling at the thought of them.

Y ou always see them with their blue noses,
O n their cute fluffy fur is their cute patches.
U and I will never stop loving the grey bears
   with the blue nose!

Alana Kerry Wallace (10)
Maud Primary School, Peterhead

Cute Cats

C ats are cute and just the best,
U nder the tables, sometimes they can be a pest!
T otally spoilt and very smart,
E veryone knows that they love cream tarts!

C ats miaow for food all day long,
A ll the time from dusk to dawn!
T ogether we're happy as we are all the time,
S o we're sitting in the sun feeling just fine!

Lisa Jane Mowat (10)
Maud Primary School, Peterhead

Cheese

C heese, cheese! Wonderful, colourful cheese,
H ow many colours can you name? Blue, orange, yellow and
mouldy green!
E veryone should love cheese.
E veryone shall love cheese!
S ometimes strong and sometimes mild,
E veryone shout, *'Cheese! Lovely cheese! Yeah!'*

Lauren Smith (10)
Maud Primary School, Peterhead

My Dogs

M y dogs are very friendly and love cuddles,
Y ou would like them, they are black, gold, soft and cute.

D igging up mole holes, chasing cats,
O n my grass they play all day.
G oing after birds flying high,
S ometimes they're funny, licking my face, *woof, woof* they say.

Connor Matthews (10)
Maud Primary School, Peterhead

Cats And Dogs

C ats are clever,
A lways out-smarting dogs
T he dogs are always chasing them!
S o they are always climbing trees to escape.

A lso the cat miaows for some food.
N ever leave a cat or dog alone!
D ogs need water and food too!

D ogs can bite when you annoy them.
'O ops, what have I done,' the dog says.
'G o away!' the people shout at the dogs.
S o be careful how you treat them!

Stephanie-Louise Wilson (9)
Maud Primary School, Peterhead

Monkeys

Monkeys -
Active, cheeky,
Swinging, playing, climbing,
Being silly with each other.
Funny!

Isla Baxter (9)
Maud Primary School, Peterhead

Sheep

S heep are so cute and cuddly.
H eat and love they need,
E specially when it's raining,
E very day and night,
P eople like them for eating, but I don't I like them for pets!

James Gordon Scott (9)
Maud Primary School, Peterhead

Mr Butter Meets Miss Milk

Mr Butter wanted some friends
And searched for them forever
He looked and looked but could not find
Some friends to last, however
One day he stopped outside a house
And looked and saw a sign
It said, *I want some friends, so please*
Come in and have some wine.
Mr Butter knocked on the door
And stood and waited long
Then finally he heard footsteps
And a very pretty song
The door opened and there she stood
A really pretty lady
Her name was Milk and then she said
'Come in and talk to me'
They talked and talked then suddenly
He got down on his knees
And said to her, 'I love you so please will you marry me?'
On their wedding day they asked
To change their name to Cheese
And after the honeymoon had passed
They settled to married life with ease
And to this day they've lived with joy
In a little cottage
So happily together
With their bouncing baby boy!

Rebecca Phelan (10)
Maud Primary School, Peterhead

Loneliness

Loneliness is light blue like tears
And sounds like sadness in the air.
It smells like no one is in the area.
Loneliness tastes like the rain from up above
And looks like a bad dream.
It reminds me of not having friends.

Koray Erdogdu (8)
Middlefield Primary School, Aberdeen

Sadness

Sadness is the colour blue.
It makes me feel alone.
My heart feels empty
And I just don't like it.
It has no taste
And feels like a blanket covering me.

Ryan Black (9)
Middlefield Primary School, Aberdeen

Fear

Fear is the colour red,
Like lightning in the sky.
It smells of rotten cheese
And tastes like stale food.
Fear is dark,
It feels like prison walls
And reminds me of bad times.

Caitlyn Stewart (9)
Middlefield Primary School, Aberdeen

Jealousy

Jealousy is black like tar.
It sounds like thunder and lightning
On a stormy day.
It feels like rotten food left in the sun
And tastes like sour milk.
Jealousy looks like a hard black rock
And feels like wet, muddy grass.
It reminds me of bad times.

Shannon McPake (8)
Middlefield Primary School, Aberdeen

Anger

Anger is red like a fiery building.
It smells like lava from a volcano.
Anger tastes of burning flames,
And sounds like the Devil screaming.
It looks like blood boiling in a pot.
Anger feels as though my heart's on fire.
It reminds me of when I was raging.

Aaron Masson (8)
Middlefield Primary School, Aberdeen

Happiness

Happiness is yellow like the sun.
It sounds like my mum laughing.
It tastes like Chalmers cakes
And looks like Mika, my dog.
It feels like a cosy bed.
It reminds me of my family.

Filip Lendzion (10)
Middlefield Primary School, Aberdeen

Silence

Silence is white like a blank sheet of paper.
It tastes like still water,
It smells like the air
And looks like an abandoned street.
It sounds like birds flying in the blue sky.
Silence feels like a ghost walking through me.

Rebecca Lowe (11)
Middlefield Primary School, Aberdeen

Sadness

Sadness is blue,
It sounds like the howling wind.
Sadness tastes like salted water
And smells of oranges.
It looks like the deep blue sea.
It feels like rain pouring down.
Sadness reminds me of being alone.

Jodie Hughes (9)
Middlefield Primary School, Aberdeen

Fear

Fear is black like a smoky tunnel.
It sounds like an eerie echo
And tastes like rotten eggs.
It smells like a garbage bin.
It looks like a misty hole.
Fear reminds me of a nightmare.

Jack Thomson (9)
Middlefield Primary School, Aberdeen

Football

Football, football is so mad,
Oh we lost, that is so sad.
On the pitch there is trouble,
They get in an awkward muddle.
Ball, ball just flies through the sky,
All the players go crazy when they score.
Living the dream isn't a bore.
Love it! It's even better when you score.

John Donald (11)
Middlefield Primary School, Aberdeen

Sadness

Sadness is blue like the morning sky.
It tastes like sour lemons one after another.
It smells like the salty sea
And looks like an upside-down smile.
It sounds like a slow song,
It feels like being squashed.
Sadness, I wish it did not exist.

Damien Genocchio (11)
Middlefield Primary School, Aberdeen

Anger

Anger is red like an apple ripe to eat.
Anger tastes like wood, hard and crunchy.
Anger smells like rotten eggs.
Anger sounds like sharp nails on the board.
Anger feels like sharp needles.
Anger is mad and makes me feel sad.

Conor Brand (11)
Middlefield Primary School, Aberdeen

Cats

I had a cat
That was fat,
Who loved watching darts in the dark.
He slept on a mat that was smart
And purred the night away.

I had a cat
That was young and smart,
His name was Bill and he was still
On the window sill.

I had a cat
That was smart
And helped me through my maths
By doing my homework tasks,
But best of all he was a copycat.

I had a cat
That was daft
And loved to go to the caf'
For a Scooby snack,
Even though he was a cat
And ate six rats after that,
But after all, he was a daft cat.

I had a cat
That was black
And had a pet bat
In a cart
With its jam tart
In the back,
Along with its sleeping cap.

Dean Barnes (11)
Middlefield Primary School, Aberdeen

The Pig With A Wig

There once was a pig
Called Rig,
Who wore a pink wig
And danced a jig.
He liked to dig
And make the hole big.
He liked to play tig
And eat lots of figs.

Stephen Fraser (11)
Middlefield Primary School, Aberdeen

My Pet Cat

My pet cat,
Young and scruffy,
Purrs, purrs, purrs,
Eats everything it can see,
Typical lazy cat.
Cute and curious,
Able to climb
Trees, trees, trees.

Connor O'Grady (12)
Middlefield Primary School, Aberdeen

No One Passes Me!

I'm a sixty-minute hacker,
I'm a left back attacker,
I'm a scrapper.
No one tackles me!

Greg Shearer (11)
Middlefield Primary School, Aberdeen

Jealousy

Jealousy is green
Like a green-eyed monster.
It smells like dirty socks
And tastes like sticky goo.
Looks dangerous like a stranger is behind you,
Feels like devils going round in your head.
It sounds like crashing waves.
Jealousy reminds me of fighting with my sister.

Rianne Gorman (9)
Middlefield Primary School, Aberdeen

Jealousy!

Jealousy is like cut green glass.
It smells like rotten food
And it tastes like acid melting in your throat.
It looks like a car crash.
Jealousy feels like jabby nettles.
It sounds like thunder and lightning
It reminds me of being *angry!*

Connor McLeod (8)
Middlefield Primary School, Aberdeen

Love

Love is blue like the sky,
It sounds like the waves on the sea.
Love smells like strawberries
And tastes of raspberries.
It looks like the sun shining
And feels like a heart full of joy.
Love reminds me of my friends.

Tafi Gaza (9)
Middlefield Primary School, Aberdeen

Sadness

Sadness is the colour grey.
Sadness is unhappy like crying.
My heart is hurting like a cut on my hand.
It has no taste as my heart is empty.
Sadness looks like a dark mist around me

Kamil Szynlklewski (9)
Middlefield Primary School, Aberdeen

Untitled

Fear is black as the sky.
It sounds like thunder.
It tastes like crusty sausages.
It looks like people falling.
It feels like worries.
It smells like eggs.
It reminds me of gunge.

Emily Russell (8)
Newhills Primary School, Aberdeen

Love

Love is red like a rose
It tastes like chocolate
It sounds like a heartbeat
It reminds me of my family
It smells like my house
It looks like my sister
It feels like a hug.

Emma Morrison (8)
Newhills Primary School, Aberdeen

Fear

Fear is black like night in the forest.
Fear smells like bins.
Fear looks angry because it sees people happy.
Fear tastes like rotten pizza.
Fear feels scary.
Fear sounds like something going in the dump.
Fear reminds me of Roger Rabbit.

Chloe Whyte (8)
Newhills Primary School, Aberdeen

Happiness

Happiness is blue like blossoming flowers,
It smells like my granny's caramel shortbread,
It sounds like birds tweeting,
It reminds me of my family,
It looks like clouds floating in the sky,
It tastes like melted chocolate,
It feels like the sun.

Erin Duncan (8)
Newhills Primary School, Aberdeen

Happiness

Happiness is yellow like the sun
It tastes like chocolate
It sounds like quietness
It reminds me of good times
It feels like you are flying high in the sky on a beautiful day
It looks like a happy smile

Rebecca Frew (8)
Newhills Primary School, Aberdeen

Untitled

Happiness is as yellow as stars up high
It looks like smiles in the sky.
It feels like a warm sunny day.
It smells like melting chocolates.
It tastes like strawberries.
It reminds me of last summer.
It sounds like giggles.

Holly Martin (8)
Newhills Primary School, Aberdeen

Untitled

Sadness is blue like the sky
Sadness tastes like tears
Sadness feels like it hurts you
Sadness looks like crying
Sadness smells like hospitals
Sadness reminds me of when
                      people are dying

Lewis Hutchison (8)
Newhills Primary School, Aberdeen

Untitled

Fear is white, like a pale frightened face,
It feels like sadness,
It sounds like thunder,
It tastes like trash,
It looks like you're scared,
It smells like a ghost
It reminds me of really scary heights.

Morgan Stephen (8)
Newhills Primary School, Aberdeen

Happiness

Happiness is yellow like the sun
It smells like my granny's cooking
It tastes like my granny's Mars bar cakes
It reminds me of when my little brother
                              and sister were born.
It looks like a fully grown sunflower
It makes me feel like hugging someone
It sounds like tweeting birds.

Thomas Davidson (8)
Newhills Primary School, Aberdeen

Untitled

Sadness is black like a dark, dark corridor
Sadness tastes like a rotten banana
Sadness feels like everyone is against you
Sadness sounds like thunder and lightning
Sadness smells like the inside of a gym shoe
Sadness looks like everything is dark and dull
Sadness reminds me of fights with my friends.

Chloe Martin (8)
Newhills Primary School, Aberdeen

Untitled

Love is red like roses
Love reminds me of my dog
Love smells like red roses,
Love looks like my mum
Love tastes like chocolates
Love feels like my dad.

Chloe Smith (8)
Newhills Primary School, Aberdeen

Untitled

Love is orange like a Cheesy Wotsit
It reminds me of happiness
It tastes like chocolate
It smells like flowers
It feels squidgy
It looks like a heart
It sounds like hearts beating.

James McIntosh (9)
Newhills Primary School, Aberdeen

Untitled

Happiness is the glow of the sun
It smells like fresh air
It sounds of giggling
It feels like a fluffy cloud
It tastes like caramel
It looks like a cute dog
It reminds me of my friends

Lewis Burt (8)
Newhills Primary School, Aberdeen

Fear

Fear is red like blood
It smells like blood
It feels like homework
It looks like thunder
It tastes like apples
It sounds like my gran's voice
It reminds me of dinosaurs.

Owen Rankine (8)
Newhills Primary School, Aberdeen

Jack Frost Is Here!

Jack Frost makes ice,
But Jack Frost is *not* nice!
He covers the ground with frost and ice,
He sprinkles frost everywhere!
There is no way he can miss a spot,
Everywhere is ice!

My fingers are nipping . . .
My toes are nipping as well!
Jack Frost is here.
It is so *very* clear!

Jack Frost is about!
I will even give you proof
There is lots of ice and frost up on my roof!

There is frost on my flowers
There are even patterns on the windows
All because of Jack Frost's *ice*!

Ruri Dickie (8)
Newtonhill Primary School, Stonehaven

Jack Frost!

Jack Frost sprinkles frost everywhere
On my car
On my roof
Even on my back garden
All of my plants have turned all white and
                                    are all stiff

When we go outside
We have to wear two pairs of socks
As he nips our toes
He covers the world in frost.

Adam Christie (8)
Newtonhill Primary School, Stonehaven

Cold Winter

Colder days.
Longer nights.
Short, freezing days,
Cold winter!

Trees having a rest . . .
Plants hanging their heads!
Trees are naked.
Cold winter!

Birds are struggling for food,
Worms dig deeper,
Squirrels are sleeping . . .
Cold winter!

You need to wear warm clothes,
You need to wear thicker jackets,
You have to wear gloves.
Cold winter!

Aria Kennedy (8)
Newtonhill Primary School, Stonehaven

Jack Frost

Today I woke up and the ground was white.
I knew Jack Frost had been last night.
On my way to school the road was as
                              shiny as diamonds.
And as white as paper.
He sprinkles frost everywhere.
Nobody likes the frost.
My mum's flowers don't even like it.
They hang their heads in disgust.

Adam Scott (8)
Newtonhill Primary School, Stonehaven

Jack Frost Is In My Garden!

Jack Frost sprinkles ice dust on my mum's flowers every night
in winter. . .
With his magic wand and his pointy fingers he makes the flowers
hang down.

And the ground is white!
It's Jack Frost all right!

He comes in the night and he comes in flight.
My mum goes mad, Jack Frost is glad
And he disappears when spring comes, till the next year.

My garden is cold when Jack Frost is around.
My mum's flowers hate Jack Frost and hang their heads in disgust!

Connor Munroe (8)
Newtonhill Primary School, Stonehaven

Signs Of Autumn

S horter days now autumn is here
I nside houses people gather round a fire
G eese fly from Iceland to Scotland
N o insects for swallows
S tags fight over female deer

O range and yellow leaves fall from trees
F rom high in the trees

A nimals like dormice hibernate
U nder the trees leaves pile up in heaps
T rees stop growing for a little while
U sually worms dig further under the ground
M ost leaves fall from the trees
N o warmth in the sun

Ryan Cruickshank (9)
Newtonhill Primary School, Stonehaven

Winter Wizard In Scotland!

Here comes the winter wizard . . .
He's coming into Scotland
As we are all sleeping he sprinkles his dust
He pops up here, he pops up there
He pops up everywhere
He's the winter wizard and coming into Scotland.

He's sprinkled dust on my car window
He's sprinkled dust on my rooftop
The next morning when I woke, I looked out
And the world had changed
Everything was white.

Murray Collie (8)
Newtonhill Primary School, Stonehaven

Autumn Is Fun

A nimals hibernate
U nder the ground worms go deeper
T he stags fight
U nder the leaves hedgehogs are hiding
M igrating swans come from Iceland
N ow the leaves are red and gold

I t is time to be cold
S uper crunchy leaves are great fun

F reezing weather
U nder the sheds dormice hibernate
N ow the days are short and cold.

Sorcha Hill (8)
Newtonhill Primary School, Stonehaven

Frosty Winter!

Short, frosty, cold days
Nights are longer.
The weather is very cold
Frosty winter!

Worms are digging deeper.
Animals are getting thicker coats.
Garden birds are struggling for food.
Frosty winter!

Children are playing in the snow.
Children are playing on their sledges.
Children are having fun in the snow!
Frosty winter

Ewan Brown (8)
Newtonhill Primary School, Stonehaven

Jack Frost Appears

Jack Frost makes ice
Jack Frost is nice
He sprinkles frost to every car . . .
And drops his magic near and far . . .
He flies around the clear blue sky
He's swooshing and swaying, way up high
He danced around on my house roof
If you come you will see the proof.

Daisy Smith (8)
Newtonhill Primary School, Stonehaven

Anger

Anger is brown like a boulder
In a booming avalanche,
It smells like burning smoke
It tastes like hot chilli,
It feels like hot lava,
It sounds like giant waves,
It looks like dirty water,
Anger makes me stamp my foot!

Euan Banks (8)
Strathburn Primary School, Inverurie

Anger

Anger is red like a big monster
It looks like a big storm
It smells like lots of smoke
Anger makes me shout a lot
It feels like a drum
It looks like a gooey monster
It sounds like a dragon
Anger makes me sad

Emma McDonald (7)
Strathburn Primary School, Inverurie

Anger

Anger is red like big angry flames,
It smells like really dirty smoke.
It sounds like big angry drums.
It looks like fierce waves.
It feels like someone has punched me.
It tastes like someone has been sick.
Anger makes me mad.

Kyle Taylor (7)
Strathburn Primary School, Inverurie

Anger

Anger is black like a storm with a tornado
It sounds like a big bang with thunder and lightning
It feels like big explosions in my head,
It tastes like goo in my mouth.
It smells like disgusting sewage,
It looks like a dinosaur with three horns.
Anger makes me kick and punch.

David Craig (7)
Strathburn Primary School, Inverurie

Anger

Anger looks like red flames,
It sounds like fireworks banging
Anger makes me very bad.
It feels like hot lava.
It smells like fire.
Anger tastes like hot rubber,
Anger is pushing someone over.

Nykita Penny
Strathburn Primary School, Inverurie

Anger

Anger is red like boiling hot lava.
It sounds like drums banging in my head.
It smells like badly rotten apples.
It tastes like hot chilli sauce soup.
It feels like you just want to explode.
Anger looks like exploding gas.
Anger makes me want to burst.

Megan Brown (7)
Strathburn Primary School, Inverurie

Anger

Anger is red like fearsome lava
It tastes like my curry is turning into burning fire
It looks like the sea on a stormy day
It smells like old smelly socks
It makes me feel sick
It sounds like a monster laughing
Anger makes me shout at my sister.

Ryan Garrett (7)
Strathburn Primary School, Inverurie

Anger

Anger is red like big balls of fire.
It smells like rotting eggs.
It sounds like a big thunderstorm.
It looks like a fierce dragon.
It feels like someone punching you.
It tastes like salty water.
Anger makes me stamp my feet.

Clare Abel (8)
Strathburn Primary School, Inverurie

Anger

Anger is red like a big cloud of smoke.
It sounds like the hard wind.
It smells like rotten cheese.
It looks like red-hot steamy flames.
It tastes like burning pepper.
It feels like a sharp needle.
Anger makes me hit my brother.

Emily Gray (7)
Strathburn Primary School, Inverurie

Anger

Anger is like red exploding dynamite,
Anger sounds like loud banging noises
Anger tastes like really spicy chilli peppers.
Anger looks like extremely strong tornadoes.
Anger feels like someone is punching me very hard.
Anger smells like burning firewood.
Anger makes me really lose my temper.

Eilidh Thomson (7)
Strathburn Primary School, Inverurie

Anger

Anger is red like a big fierce bull
It sounds like a fiery dragon
It smells like a huge bowl of hot chilli sauce
It looks like a hungry bull
It feels like a hard rock
It tastes like out of date juice
Anger makes my face go red.

Jade Strachan (7)
Strathburn Primary School, Inverurie

Anger

Anger is red like burning fire
It sounds like horrible gas
It looks like a big monster
It feels very gooey
It tastes like a smelly horrible drink
Anger makes me cross.

Rikki Russell (7)
Strathburn Primary School, Inverurie

Anger

Anger is red like hot fire
Anger makes my face go red.
It feels like a really hard punch.
It sounds like loud thunder.
It tastes like very hot chilli.
It looks like a really angry dragon.
It smells like a big bowl of out of date cheese.
Anger makes people really mad.

Cameron McLennan (7)
Strathburn Primary School, Inverurie

Anger

Anger is purple like an angry monster
It feels like hot chillies
It smells like burning food
Anger sounds like people shouting at me
It tastes like burning lava in my mouth
It looks like fire
Anger makes me shout loudly.

Paisley Howitt (7)
Strathburn Primary School, Inverurie

Anger

Anger is red like a bad, fierce dragon.
It looks like a swirly whirlwind.
It smells like bad-tempered smoke.
It tastes like boiling hot sauce.
It sounds like a lion about to do an enormous roar.
Anger makes me shake my fist.

Craig Allan (8)
Strathburn Primary School, Inverurie

Anger

Anger is red like the pounding heart inside of me.
It sounds like big bass drums in my head.
It smells like choking grey smoke.
It feels like I have just been shot with a poisonous arrow.
It tastes like sour lemons
It looks like a stormy sea of blood.
Anger makes me cross my arms and shout.
But I think being happy is lots more fun!

Chloe Niamh Clark (7)
Strathburn Primary School, Inverurie

Anger

Anger is green like a big, fierce, hungry dinosaur.
It tastes like hot spicy sauce.
It feels like you're out of control.
It looks like a terrible storm.
It smells like a dragon's breath.
I can hear it thumping in my head.
Anger makes me turn my back on someone.

Beth Alexander (8)
Strathburn Primary School, Inverurie

Anger

Anger is like a big fat monster.
It sounds like a thundering river.
It smells like car smoke.
It looks like burning gases.
It feels like a horrid dragon.
It tastes like a solid devil.
Anger makes me hit my big brother.

Katie Grant (7)
Strathburn Primary School, Inverurie

Anger

Anger is red like crashing fireworks.
It sounds like flashing lightning.
When I am angry it makes me feel like
                        kicking something over.
It looks like a giant exploding volcano.
It tastes like out of date cheese.
It smells like grey smoke.
Anger makes me shout.

Hollie Douglas (6)
Strathburn Primary School, Inverurie

Anger

Anger is red like a big ball of fire
It sounds like a snake hissing terribly
It smells like a rotten banana
It looks like a big ball of burning lava
It feels like a hard rock
It tastes like a big puff of smoke
Anger makes me give my pillow a big punch.

Marc Mowat (7)
Strathburn Primary School, Inverurie

Anger

Anger is red like a fierce brown bull
Anger makes me lose control of myself.
It tastes like a smelly rat.
It feels like very hard ice.
It looks like a rotten apple.
It sounds like a very loud flooded river.
Anger makes me shout.

Gary Moir (8)
Strathburn Primary School, Inverurie

Anger

Anger is like red-hot flames.
It sounds like loud banging.
It smells like mouldy cheese.
It looks like the dark.
It feels like someone is punching.
It tastes like rotten bananas.
Anger makes me kick and shout.

Jgordenna Grant (8)
Strathburn Primary School, Inverurie

To A Stag

In a quiet forest glade
A noble stag was eating bark
Where when young
He had once played.

He walked among the trees
His feet crunching on the leaves
Then letting out a warning cry
A red breasted robin flew by.

The birds flew out of the trees
The other animals bolted making a breeze.

Then a shot rang out

People then began to shout
The smell of hunters made him turn
The glint of a gun
Made him run
Towards the sun.

For he knew that the glare
Would be too much for them to bear
Then he galloped into the trees
And the stag knew that they would not get their fees

He stopped and began to eat bark
He stopped to listen to a lark.

Ian Leahy (9)
Tarland Primary School, Tarland

Eviction

We saw the burning houses in our little village.
We thought our house was next.
In the distance the Factor was coming.
We saw heavy smoke rising.

I heard the horses galloping towards us.
We heard the snapping of timber.
I felt fear in my body.
We felt the coldness of the morning.

We felt the coldness turn into the heat,
of the fire from others houses.
We could taste the smoke through our lungs.

I can still remember that day.
When I saw those men coming with those hammers.
I thought it was the end so we left before they came.
Looking back we saw a flame grow from
the wood in our house.

We ran from our village in terror never to return.
I can still smell the smoke from the eviction
even now.

James Swan (9) & Alex Vicca (10)
Westhill Primary School, Westhill

My Friend

Friends are always there for you.
Through trouble, problems and worries too.

Friends are kind and generous.
Friends are thoughtful and mostly honest.

The opposite to friends are foes.
Everybody ought to know.

They're really caring, kind and polite.
To be honest they're just right!

Jasmine Foubister (9)
Westhill Primary School, Westhill

A Friend Is

Friends are F orgiving
Friends are R eliable
Friends are I maginative
Friends are E nergetic
Friends are N ice, Ooops I mean fabulous
Friends are D elicate
Friends are S illy when they are.

So friends are Adventurous, Polite,
Beautiful, Mannerable,
Crazy, Optimistic,
Generous, Quality,
Honourable, Zany
Joyful, Wonderful,
Kind-hearted, Vital,
Laughable, Truthful,
Sympathetic and
Understandable

Morbheinn Nicol (9)
Westhill Primary School, Westhill

Friends

What is a friend?
Friends can help you
Friends can bug you.

Friends will play with you
Friends won't kick you.

Friends do well together
Friends don't lie.

Friends should trust you
Friends shouldn't laugh at you.

Friends aren't bullies
They are the best.

James Mackay (9)
Westhill Primary School, Westhill

Eviction Poem

We lived a happy life in the Highlands.
But we were soon to be evicted.
I had found a note pinned to our door.
I felt anger burn in my body.
I couldn't help but utter curses.
I ran to my dad with my feet bruised by sandy turf.
The day came, the wicked Factor with the mighty men.
We all begged for mercy, my father fighting a losing battle.
The sly Factor ignored all of our desperate cries
and set our house alight.
The flames grew like a plant.
The air grew murky and the rain began to fall.
All that was left of our house was a few stones.

The evil Factor rode away and snarled at us.

We looked at what once was our possessions, all piled
up like a junk heap.
My mother sobbed her heart out but we must now look forward.

David Copeland (9) & James Skinner (10)
Westhill Primary School, Westhill

Friends

F riends are nice to you
R eal friends will not bully you
 I f you have a friend you sometimes argue.
E very day friends meet
N ot everyone finds it easy to find friends,
D o not blackmail friends.
S ensitive friends are not too sensitive to their pals,
H appy, jolly friends play with you,
 I f you have a friend you should trust them,
P olite friends have some decent manners.

Andrew Wright (8)
Westhill Primary School, Westhill

Eviction Poem

As the sun rises we hear the birds singing a melody to
awaken my family,
Suddenly we hear horses galloping down the dusty lane
like a thunder cloud.
Then we hear a powerful knock at the door,
We opened the door and in barged Patrick Sellar with his comrades.

My poor mother,
I can just picture her tears,
Heartbroken as she hears a smash from her beautiful china plates
being thrown to the ground.
In fact all of our furniture was thrown out and ruined,
As this was happening we felt like our lives had been smashed too.
That day, that awful day, we will never forget it!

Patrick Sellar's comrades burned the house down,
But my mum refused to leave the chair in the home she was born in.

I went running in to pull my mother out of the house,
Her legs were weak and she could hardly move because the smoke
had got into her lungs.

My father and brother had worked for hour upon hours,
Day upon day, to build this house just for it to be burned to the ground!

I am 94 now and I live in Canada with my family,
I still remember that day like it was yesterday.

Holly Alexander & Rachel Black (10)
Westhill Primary School, Westhill

Friends

F riends are fun.
R are to find.
I n the world I am sure there are some.
E nough for everyone to have one.
N o one should be left out.
D ay after day your friends will play.
S o you and they are happy.

Kirsty McDonald (8)
Westhill Primary School, Westhill

Eviction

Today was the day the horsemen came,
With the infamous Factor and axes sharp as sharks teeth.
I could hear the thumping and pounding of the
horses drawing nearer.
I could feel the rising anger of the intimidating
infamous factor.
He was there outside my door bashing on the sturdy wooden door.
I could feel the house shaking.
My mother froze, she wouldn't move, I think she was in shock,
They threw out our tables, chairs and our oatmeal box.
They were all broken and shattered
The precious china had crashed into unfixable pieces,
Like our lives ruined.
They threw up matches, so the thatch went up in flames,
They were laughing, watching our hopes and dreams crumble,
I could smell the smell of the smoke rising high into the air.
Our house burning down,
We couldn't do anything about it.
They wouldn't listen to my mother's sobs or our worthless cries,
That's it, our lives and homes have gone up in smoke.
Destroyed.

Claire Bruce & Sam Williams (10)
Westhill Primary School, Westhill

Friends

F riends share sweets
R are to find
I have good friends
E verytime.
N ever lie
D o nothing bad
S hares things out
H elp when they are sad
I have good friends
P olite friends are nice to you.

Callum Craig (9)
Westhill Primary School, Westhill

Friendship

F riends are fantastic
R are and they share
I nteresting, amazing and cool
E veryday in May I play
N ever say nasty words
D on't run away just stay where you are
S haring and polite they are
H elpful and caring too
I n the day I play
P olite my friends are.

Searlait Thom (8)
Westhill Primary School, Westhill

Friends

Friends care, friends share.
They are always there for you
Friends help you when you are in trouble
They are worth it
When you are in trouble call for a friend
You will see a difference
Me and my friends play in the park
We play at school
We play after school
I love it.

Lewis Williamson (8)
Westhill Primary School, Westhill

Friends

Friends stay together for ever and ever.
Friends don't swear and stay in a pair.
Friends could stay in a bunch and do not punch.
Friends stay together and play together.

Stuart Wright (8)
Westhill Primary School, Westhill

Friendship

F riends are funny
R ight from the start
I am a good friend
E arly in the morning I play with my friends
N ever cheat
D oing football together
S o have some fun
H elpful when I am stuck
I care about my friends
P olite friends are cool.

Gavin Ritchie (9)
Westhill Primary School, Westhill

Friendship

F riends are
R eally hard to find
I have three friends
E veryday I see my friends,they
N ever tell lies
D on't bully your friends
S hare your toys with them
H onest friends are good friends
I have good friends who are
P olite friends.

Sam Steel (8)
Westhill Primary School, Westhill

Friends Forever!

Friends are nice, caring like mice,
They will help you in whatever you do,
If you are down friends are like the crown,
You will need to be very nice to be a friend,
Be friends till the very end!

Alakbar Zeynalzade (9)
Westhill Primary School, Westhill

Eviction

As the sun rises we hear the birds
singing a melody to awaken my family.
Suddenly we hear horses galloping down the dusty lane
like a thundercloud.
Then a powerful knock at the door.

We opened the door to find Patrick Seller and a few other strong men
standing there with weapons.
Patrick Seller spoke loud and clear,
'Five weeks has passed so get out now.'
We refused so they walked in
and threw our belongings and ourselves out.

While we sat on the ground sobbing
they were burning our house.
The smoke left us coughing like we had chest infections.
They left afterwards and the next morning
we left on our long, tiring journey to Glasgow.

Shannon Adie & Rachael Ronald (10)
Westhill Primary School, Westhill

A Good Friend

Friends can help
Friends can't be mean.

Friends will play and chat with you
Friends won't run away.

Friends do nice things
Friends don't upset you.

Friends should cheer you up
Friends shouldn't dare you to do anything.

Friends aren't nasty and horrible
They are there for you and full of *love*.

Emma Stanley (8)
Westhill Primary School, Westhill

Eviction

It was an unfortunate day
When the horrifying Patrick Seller
Came stomping to our door

They kicked the door open with a *bang!*
Charging at us like a stampede
We pleaded with them to give us more time.

They threw our possessions out
With no respect
They broke our china
We cried and cried
We heard the crumbing sound of the rocks.

The slam of the furniture
On the crumbling stones
We smelt smoke in the air
Of the thin sky.

I sniffed with disgust
We felt like we were leaving
The world when we left
Culmailie in The Highlands

Cameron Macdonald & Raymond Aina (9)
Westhill Primary School, Westhill

Friends

F riends are kind
R eal helpful
I hate telling tales
E verytime you get hurt they help you
N ever bully people
D on't swear
S hare toys
H elping out
I like friends
P laying brings happy times.

Callum Ridley (8)
Westhill Primary School, Westhill

Eviction Poem

It was morning, I had just woken up from a delightful sleep
I looked out the door at the beautiful shining sun rising above
                                    the marvellous, green hillside
But then I heard the thundering of horse's hooves against the dirty,
                                    brown, country track
It was time.
Patrick Seller had come to force us out of our beloved country home
I felt anger building up inside my body
Not a long wait after there was a knocking at our old, wooden door
The door flung open violently and Patrick Seller stormed in

Those two words he uttered are still echoing inside my head
Get out!
He started flinging old furniture out of our muddy, wooden doorway
The other man started grabbing my mother, she was struggling
frantically
She picked herself up and ran back in to save her beloved china
Soon after she was back outside
Her beautiful china was smashed beside her

I was watching from underneath my ripped, tattered blanket
Soon the thatch above my head caught fire
Smoke started to fill my lungs. The only sound I could hear
was my mother desperately wailing my name
Alfie Alfie!
I could feel the heat on my skin
It was becoming harder to breathe
I ran out of my blackhouse I used to call home
I just got out in time to see my home as a big pile of stones
My home in Dornoch is no more
I know I can never go back
My heart will always belong there.

Abbie Houston & Emily Berry (10)
Westhill Primary School, Westhill

Eviction

It was a tragic day when we heard the horses galloping towards
our house.
They knocked on the door and then they kicked it down
Our hearts were thumping very fast.
They had a sledgehammer and an axe.
We were terrified and scared, where would we live?
They were smashing up the furniture with loud crashes.
They lit the thatch and the smoke was overpowering.
The smoke had a bitter taste.
The smell was absolutely awful.
It touched our lungs, making us cough terribly.
We went outside and saw the other house burning and heard
the horses galloping away.
We felt broken and bashed. What will the future have in store for us?

Daniel Wood & Ryan Smith (10)
Westhill Primary School, Westhill

Friendship

F riends care for you.
R ight when you need them.
I nstead of having a fight you are nice to one another.
E very day you enjoy with your friends.
N ever have a fight with a friend.
D o play very nicely.
S o a friend is someone who cares for you.
H aving a friend should cheer you up.
I f you dared a friend to do something bad they might break
friends with you.
P eople can be friends with everyone.

Rhys Williams (8)
Westhill Primary School, Westhill

Eviction

The Countess of Sutherland
arrived with her men and horses.
She struck the door
with a heavy loud knock
but nobody answered
so she knocked again
but this time even louder.
She knew that we would
have heard her that time.

She had had enough
so she got her men to
kick the door down.
They came storming in at us
at the speed of light.
She told us to get out
at the count of ten.
At this moment I felt like
running over to them
and strangling them to death
but I knew that if I did
I would get hurt, so I didn't.

We stood our ground.
She said that if we didn't
get out of the house
she would burn us alive.
We quickly dashed out
of the house, taking our
belongings and we stood
rooted to the ground
watching our house burn down.

Walking away in tears
we started the long walk
over the mountains.
We didn't have a clue
what lay ahead of us.

Sam Kelsey & Sam Hibbard (9)
Westhill Primary School, Westhill

Eviction

After a day's warning they came in haste
Patrick Seller and his vast army of men were coming.
I heard their horses canter across the road.
The family were horrified because they knew what was
                                        going to happen.

Patrick Seller screamed at the family.
He was going to knock the house down.
Everyone was absolutely fearful.
You could smell the ashes' flare.

You could hear the china crack.
You could smell the natural air turning into smoke.
My mother wept and the tears tumbled.
I could see the flames blink.
My sister was panic-stricken.
The noise of the table legs was like thunder
And I could taste fear
And the peat biting at you hands as the roof was falling in.

I am dying now
And my enchanting child
Tells the story
Of what happened to me.

Ali Hashemizadeh & Callum Chapman (9)
Westhill Primary School, Westhill

Friends Are The Best Of All

Friends are the best
they do not use you
to cheat on tests.

They play with you
and never
let you down.

If your friends
shout out or are self-centred
they are not a friend.

Everyone should have a friend.
Friends are the best
the best of all.

Sally Cuthbertson (8)
Westhill Primary School, Westhill

True Friends

F riends can
R eally help.
I n the playground they play with you.
E very friend should be nice.
N ice friends are true friends.
D on't let people bully your friends.
S ome friends are cool.
H elp your friends.
I like my friends.
P lay with your friends.

Rhys Mennie (8)
Westhill Primary School, Westhill

What Is A Friend!

Friends can be kind
Friends can't be mean.

Friends will play with you
Friends won't tease others.

Friends do care for you
Friends don't tell tales.

Friends should be honest
Friends shouldn't be bossy.

Friends aren't selfish
They are funny!

Megan MacDonald (9)
Westhill Primary School, Westhill

Friendship

F riends are the best in the world.
R eady for fun the next day.
I nside the playhouse.
E verlasting friends forever.
N ever breaking up for days and days.
D ancing and singing, having pop star fun.
S winging on the swing
H aving lots of fun
I n the corridor way
P lanning to play another day!

Marieke Maliepaard (8)
Westhill Primary School, Westhill

What Is A Friend

Friends can help you
Friends can't hurt you
Friends will play with you
Friends won't run away
Friends do nice things
Friends don't bully each other
Friends should, be kind
Friends shouldn't be bossy
Friends aren't bad
Friends are good.

Lewis McPherson
Westhill Primary School, Westhill

Friend

F riends are fun just like mine
R eally cool are my friends
I ncredibly nice are my friends
E xciting and fun are my friends
N othing can stop them playing with me
D on't be unkind, don't be my enemy
S hare things my friends do
H elpful to me are my friends
I really like my friends help
P lease be a good friend.

Amber Love (8)
Westhill Primary School, Westhill

Caring About Friends

F riends are nice to each other
R eally nice to each other
I n school they do not shout at you
E very time you are hurt they help you
N ever, ever be nasty to your friends
D o things together and play together
S hare stuff and tell secrets.
H elp to make things
I n the end they talk to each other
P lease be my friend.

Daniel Bannerman (8)
Westhill Primary School, Westhill

Friendship Poem

F riends
R eally help a lot
I n play they play a lot with you.
E very friend should be
N ice
D on't let people bully your friends.
S ome friends are kind.
H appy friends are really nice.
I n general friends are really generous.
P lay with your friends.

Daniel Hay (8)
Westhill Primary School, Westhill

Highland Eviction

We can hear the sound of the hooves
We know the Factor and his men are coming
So many people are sobbing
The Factor and his men are throwing out our precious furniture,
Setting alight our humble home
I wonder where we will go to find a new home
My mother wailed with a tear in her eye,
Where shall we go?
Am I going to die?
The men put locks on the door once the burning had stopped.

We slept in a cave with horrid memories of the day before
It was dark, damp and smelly and we wanted our old home
back, even though the smell of smoke was still strong in the air
What shall we do?
All our furniture is lying in a sad broken heap in the dirt
And our irreplaceable china is smashed.

A year has passed since the eviction,
But memories are still powerful in our minds
Our old life was much better than city life in Glasgow,
Comparing farming in fresh air
To a smoky mill
I feel sorry for us all
Oh why did it have to be us?

Jamie Horgan & Ewan Murphy (9)
Westhill Primary School, Westhill

Eviction Poem

We could hear the horses from miles away.
We looked over the hill and we saw smoke.
Oh my it was Patrick Seller with his men.
We had to get packed or leave because he was
Despicable
Patrick Seller's coming, what's he gonna do? He's gonna
knock the door down.
He threw me but my mum would not move, he burnt
our house I had to get my mum so she came out
because of me.
I came back as an old man and saw the remains of
the house.

Sean Reid & Fraser Middleton (10)
Westhill Primary School, Westhill

Friendship!

Friends are fun
Rare and sometimes glum
I like to share
Everywhere
Nothing stops friendship
Don't let people bully your friends
Silly friends are not fun to play with
I don't like my enemies
Please be someone's friend.

Melanie Alexander (8)
Westhill Primary School, Westhill

Young Writers Information

We hope you have enjoyed reading this
book - and that you will continue to enjoy it
in the coming years.

If you like reading and writing poetry drop
us a line, or give us a call, and we'll send
you a free information pack.

Alternatively if you would like to order
further copies of this book or any of our
other titles, then please give us a call or
log onto our website at
www.youngwriters.co.uk

**Young Writers Information
Remus House
Coltsfoot Drive
Peterborough
PE2 9JX**

(01733) 890066